boilerplate: D0362907

A UNIQUE CHILD SERIES

Keeping Safe

Being safe and protected ■ Discovering boundaries ■ Making choices

by Liz Wilcock

Published by Practical Pre-School Books, A Division of MA Education Ltd, St Jude's Church, Dulwich Road, Herne Hill, London, SE24 0PB.

Tel: 020 7738 5454 www.practicalpreschoolbooks.com

© MA Education Ltd 2014

Design: Alison Cutler fonthillcreative 01722 717043

All images © MA Education Ltd. All photos taken by Lucie Carlier.

ISBN 978-1-909280-69-4

Introduction:
Keeping Safe

'Unique' is a word that has been firmly associated with the Early Years Foundation Stage (EYFS) since 2008. As the first of the four theme headings, the term 'unique child' has come to represent everything about a child, in other words – All About Me!

The revised EYFS framework, which became effective from September 2012, has taken forward the Government's reforms to the original 2008 framework. Recommendations in the 2011 Tickell Review had a focus on strengthening partnerships between parents and professionals in the best interests of each child and this is a crucial element within the 'Unique Child' theme.

Many define the word 'unique' as 'being an individual', but what does this broadly mean within the EYFS and, specifically, for the child?

Before we explore this, it is worth reminding ourselves of the EYFS principle and commitments for A Unique Child.

Principle

Every child is a competent learner from birth who can be resilient, capable, confident and self-assured.

Commitments

1.1 Child Development
Babies and children develop in individual ways and at varying rates. Every area of development – physical, cognitive, linguistic, spiritual, social and emotional – is equally important.

1.2 Inclusive Practice
The diversity of individuals and communities is valued and respected. No child or family is discriminated against.

1.3 Keeping Safe
Young children are vulnerable. They develop resilience when their physical and psychological well-being is protected by adults.

1.4 Health and Well-being
Children's health is an integral part of their emotional, mental, social, environmental and spiritual well-being and is supported by attention to these aspects.

So, what does all of this mean for a child? Without doubt, if a child is respected, supported in his/her learning, happy, emotionally secure and well loved, the child will thrive throughout their early years.

When children recognise that key people in their lives are responsive to their care and learning needs, that these people are looking out for them to keep them safe and healthy, the impact on the children will be positive.

Children need to know who they are, and will need support to affirm aspects of their own identities. To understand how each child is unique, we can think about ourselves – how do we know that we are unique? What makes us unique?

Whether we consider aspects such as our own appearance, what we think about ourselves or how others view us – all of these things will describe our uniqueness – that is, what makes us an individual.

It is important for children to understand and appreciate their own identity, that is, to know their name, date of birth, whether they are male or female, the colour of their skin and their own physical features. In addition, children need to know the composition of their family and where they are in relation to their siblings. When children develop a strong sense of identity, individually and within a group, they will gain a sense of belonging. The role of the adult is to support each child to become comfortable with themselves, to be assertive and self assured.

This book is about the third commitment of A Unique Child – Keeping Safe.

We will explore ways to keep children safe from harm, recognising that babies and children are vulnerable as they have little sense of danger and only learn to assess risks with help from adults. Striking a balance between a child's safety and being overprotective is important – being overprotected may prevent children from learning about possible dangers and about how to protect themselves from harm, whether this harm stems from within the environment or though abusive treatment from others.

We will consider how we can introduce boundaries to young children – how we can involve parents in the process of using a consistent approach when helping children learn right from wrong. We need to help children to understand why we all live with rules and boundaries – we are helping them to understand that there are consequences to our actions.

In supporting children to make choices, we will consider how we can help them to understand that while there may be several different options to choose from, they can only choose one at a time. As children learn to make choices, they feel that they have some sense of control over their day and of course some choices are not about what a child wants to do but what they may choose not to do.

Young children are vulnerable – they need to develop trust in the adults who are responsible for them. When children are treated kindly and with respect, they flourish. When emphasis is placed on keeping children safe in childcare settings, parents need continuous reassurance that their children are fully protected. The adults are responsible for managing children's behaviour in an appropriate way, to help each child understand the why we may need to say 'no' sometimes.

The role of the adult is crucial – from assessing risks in the environment to recognising signs that a child may be at risk of harm from others – the practitioner must be vigilant at all times.

Section 1:
Being safe and protected

The Statutory Framework (2014) Department for Education

'This framework is for all early years providers (from 1 September 2014): maintained schools; non-maintained schools; independent schools; all providers on the Early Years Register; and all providers registered with an early years childminder agency. The learning and development requirements are given legal force by an Order made under Section 39(1)(a) of the Childcare Act 2006. The safeguarding and welfare requirements are given legal force by Regulations made under Section 39(1)(b) of the Childcare Act 2006'.

The Framework makes clear what you must do to keep children safe from harm.

'Ofsted has regard to the Early Years Foundation Stage (EYFS) in carrying out inspections, and reports on the quality and standards of provision. Ofsted may issue a notice to improve (in respect of any failure to meet a requirement in the document), and/or may issue a welfare requirements notice. It is an offence for a provider to fail to comply with a welfare requirements notice'.

The Safeguarding and Welfare Requirements cover the steps that providers must take to keep children safe and promote their welfare.

The Statutory Framework states that 'children learn best when they are healthy, safe and secure, when their individual needs are met, and when they have positive relationships with the adults caring for them. The safeguarding and welfare requirements are designed to help providers create high quality settings which are welcoming, safe and stimulating, and where children are able to enjoy learning and grow in confidence. Providers must take all necessary steps to keep children safe and well'.

So, what are the Safeguarding and Welfare Requirements that relate to keeping children safe?

There are two broad areas for us to consider: protecting children from abuse (child protection) and keeping children safe within the environment.

Child protection

The framework states that you must be alert to any issues for concern in the child's life at home or elsewhere. You must also have and implement a policy, and have procedures in place, to safeguard children. These should be in line with the guidance and procedures of the relevant Local Safeguarding Children Board (LSCB). The safeguarding policy and procedures must include an explanation of the action to be taken in the event of an allegation being made against a member of staff, and cover the use of mobile phones and cameras in the setting.

A practitioner must be designated to take lead responsibility for safeguarding children in every setting. Childminders must take the lead responsibility themselves. The lead practitioner is responsible for liaison with local statutory children's services agencies, and with the LSCB. They must provide support, advice and guidance to any other staff on an ongoing basis, and on any specific safeguarding issue as required. The lead practitioner must attend a child protection training course that enables them to identify, understand and respond appropriately to signs of possible abuse and neglect.

Providers of childcare must train all staff to understand their safeguarding policy and procedures, and ensure that all staff have up to date knowledge of safeguarding issues. Training must enable staff to identify signs of possible abuse and neglect at the earliest opportunity, and to respond in a timely and appropriate way. These may include:

● significant changes in children's behaviour;

● deterioration in children's general well-being;

● unexplained bruising, marks or signs of possible abuse or neglect;

● children's comments which give cause for concern;

● any reasons to suspect neglect or abuse outside the setting, for example in the child's home; and/or

● inappropriate behaviour displayed by other members of staff, or any other person working with the children, for example, inappropriate sexual comments, excessive one-to-one attention beyond the requirements of their usual role and responsibilities, or inappropriate sharing of images.

You must have regard to the Government's statutory guidance 'Working Together to Safeguard Children 2013' (www.gov.uk/government/publications/working-together-to-safeguard-children).

If a setting has concerns about children's safety or welfare, they must notify agencies with statutory responsibilities without delay. This means the local children's social care services and, in emergencies, the police.

Registered providers must inform Ofsted, or their childminder agency, of any allegations of serious harm or abuse by any person living, working, or looking after children at the premises (whether the allegations relate to harm or abuse committed on the premises or elsewhere). The setting must also notify Ofsted or their childminder agency of the action taken in respect of the allegations. These notifications must be made as soon as is reasonably practicable, but at the latest within 14 days of the allegations being made. It is important to remember that a setting, without reasonable excuse, that fails to comply with this requirement, commits an offence.

Every setting must also meet their responsibilities under the Safeguarding Vulnerable Groups Act 2006, which includes a duty to make a referral to the Disclosure and Barring Service where a member of staff is dismissed (or would

have been, had the person not left the setting first) because they have harmed a child or put a child at risk of harm.

Disqualification

(This applies to all registered providers and employees in registered settings).

It is an offence for someone registered to provide childminding or childcare to knowingly employ someone who is disqualified.

A person may be disqualified if they, or a person who lives with them, has been:

- found to have committed a relevant offence against a child;

- made subject to an order or determination removing a child from their care or preventing a child from living with them;

- found to have committed certain offences against an adult; for example, murder, kidnapping, rape, indecent assault, or assault causing actual bodily harm;

- charged with certain offences against an adult, or an

offence that is related to an offence, and had a relevant order imposed;

- included on the list of those who are barred from working with children, held by the Independent Safeguarding Authority;

- made the subject of a disqualifying order;

- refused registration as a childcarer previously or have had registration cancelled, unless the cancellation was only for non-payment of fees for continued registration after 1 September 2008;

- refused registration as a provider or manager of children's homes or have had registration cancelled.

Providers must notify Ofsted of any significant event which is likely to affect the suitability of any person who is in regular contact with children on the premises where childcare is provided. The disqualification of an employee could be an instance of a significant event.

(Sources: Ofsted www.ofsted.gov.uk, Department for Education, www.gov.uk)

The environment: safety and suitability of premises and equipment

Safety

Adults must ensure that the premises, including overall floor space and outdoor spaces, are fit for purpose and suitable for the age of children cared for and the activities provided on the premises. Adults must comply with requirements of health and safety legislation, including fire safety and hygiene requirements.

Adults must also take reasonable steps to ensure the safety of children, staff and others on the premises in the case of fire or any other emergency, and must have an emergency evacuation procedure. In addition, adults must have appropriate fire detection and control equipment (for example, fire alarms, smoke detectors, fire blankets and/ or fire extinguishers) which need to be in working order. Fire exits must be clearly identifiable, and fire doors must be free of obstruction and easily opened from the inside.

Premises

The premises and equipment must be organised in a way that meets the needs of children.

The premises should be well ventilated and have suitable heating for the winter months. The maintenance of property and equipment is important, to ensure that the children can have a safe place to play.

Staff must ensure that wet floors do not present a slipping hazard for the children, parents, visitors or themselves. They need to make sure that drawers are closed when not in use and that any free standing cabinets are not top heavy as they could topple over. Fire doors should never be wedged open.

Providers must follow their legal responsibilities under the Equality Act 2010, for example, the provisions on reasonable adjustments.

Adults must provide access to an outdoor play area or, if that is not possible, ensure that outdoor activities are planned and taken on a daily basis, unless circumstances make this inappropriate, for example unsafe weather conditions.

Provision must be made (space or partitioned area) for children who wish to relax, play quietly or sleep, equipped with appropriate furniture. Sleeping children must be frequently checked. Except in childminding settings, there should be a separate baby room for children under the age of two. However, adults must ensure that younger

Something to think about

O   Electrical cords should not be within reach of children. Provide socket covers so that there are no exposed wall sockets.

O   A list of emergency phone numbers needs to be posted near each telephone in the setting.

O   Any large tubs/buckets/paddling pools containing water need to be closely supervised and emptied when not in use since small amounts of water can be a drowning hazard for young children.

O   Ensure that there are no poisonous plants on the premises.

O   All toys need to be safe by being age and stage appropriate for the children in the group.

Risk assessment

Each adult must ensure that they take all reasonable steps to ensure children in their care are not exposed to risks and must be able to demonstrate how they are managing risks. Discussions are necessary to help determine where it may be helpful to make some written risk assessments in relation to specific issues, to inform staff practice, and to demonstrate how the staff team are managing risks, if asked by parents and/or carers or inspectors. Risk assessments should identify aspects of the environment that need to be checked on a regular basis, when and by whom those aspects will be checked, and how the risk will be removed or minimised.

Outings

Children must be kept safe while on outings. Adults must assess the risks or hazards which may arise for the children, and must identify the steps to be taken to remove, minimise and manage those risks and hazards. The assessment must include consideration of adult to child ratios. The risk assessment does not necessarily need to be in writing; this is for the adults to decide on. Vehicles in which children are being transported, and the driver of those vehicles, must be adequately insured. When children are due to be taken out, for example, to the local park, older children may contribute to the discussion on what needs to be thought about before they leave the setting. Children love to be a part of a 'plan'!

Accident or injury

Settings must ensure there is a first aid box accessible at all times with appropriate content for use with children – the adults must keep a written record of accidents or injuries and first aid treatment and must inform parents and/or carers of any accident or injury sustained by the child on the same day, or as soon as reasonably practicable, of any first aid treatment given.

As a guide to what could be included in a first aid box, the Health and Safety Executive provide the following information on their website – hse.gov.uk.

'As a guide, where work activities involve low hazards, a minimum stock of first-aid items might be:

● a leaflet giving general guidance on first aid, for example, HSE's leaflet Basic advice on first aid at work);

● 20 individually wrapped sterile plasters (assorted sizes), appropriate to the type of work (hypoallergenic plasters can be provided if necessary);

children in a baby room have contact with older children and are moved into the older age group when appropriate. An example of this could be at mealtimes when older children and babies can come together to mix socially, along with the adults responsible for them.

Providers must ensure there is an adequate number of toilets and hand basins available (usually one toilet and one hand basin for every ten children over the age of two). Except in childminding settings, there should usually be separate toilet facilities for adults. There must be suitable hygienic changing facilities for changing any children who are in nappies and adults should ensure that an adequate supply of clean bedding, towels, spare clothes and any other necessary items is always available.

There must be an area where staff may talk to parents and/or carers confidentially, as well as an area in group settings for staff to take breaks away from areas being used by children.

The adults must only release children into the care of individuals who have been notified to the setting by the parent, and must ensure that children do not leave the premises unsupervised. In addition, the adults must take all reasonable steps to prevent unauthorised persons entering the premises, and have an agreed procedure for checking the identity of visitors.

Providers must carry public liability insurance. Inspectors will check that current insurance is in place and displayed in the setting. The insurance needs to be tailored to the individual business to ensure that appropriate cover is in place.

SECTION 1: BEING SAFE AND PROTECTED

- two sterile eye pads;

- two individually wrapped triangular bandages, preferably sterile;

- six safety pins;

- two large sterile individually wrapped unmedicated wound dressings;

- six medium-sized sterile individually wrapped unmedicated wound dressings;

- at least three pairs of disposable gloves.

Registered providers must notify Ofsted of any serious accident, illness or injury to, or death of, any child while in their care, and of the action taken. Notification must be made as soon as is reasonably practicable, but in any event within 14 days of the incident occurring. A registered provider, who, without reasonable excuse, fails to comply with this requirement, commits an offence. Providers must notify local child protection agencies of any serious accident or injury to, or the death of, any child while in their care, and must act on any advice from those agencies.

(Sources: Ofsted www.ofsted.gov.uk, Department for Education, www.gov.uk, www.hse.gov.uk)

Ultimately, the role of the adult is to keep children safe. Staff should always be taking steps to minimise risk for the children. In this section of the book, we will consider how you can protect children from harm in terms of child protection.

When we hear about injuries or deaths involving children, we must let this stay as a reminder to us all about the responsibility we have in ensuring the safety and wellbeing of every child.

The priority of adults working with children is to ensure that the needs and safety of each child is always put first. Professionals should, whenever possible, work with parents to keep their children safe. The role of the key person in the setting cannot be underestimated – getting to know the child and the family well is important. The key person should develop sound professional relationships with the family in the best interests of the child. If there are concerns about a child's welfare, the key person will play a crucial part in any investigation.

There are four categories of abuse that adults working with children need to be aware of:

- Physical;

- Sexual;

- Emotional; and

- Neglect.

Although these categories describe the different ways in which children may be harmed, they may also combine, for example, if a child was harmed in a sexual or physical way, emotionally that child would be suffering too. It is important that every practitioner recognises the signs of abuse.

Physical abuse is non-accidental injury – deliberately inflicted. This can include: hitting, shaking, squeezing, burns, bruising, broken limbs, cuts, bites, gripping, giving a child inappropriate drugs or alcohol and attempting to poison, suffocate or drown.

Physical abuse can cause long term problems – scars, internal injuries, brain damage – even death in extreme situations.

Of course, children may accidentally harm themselves as they play and explore. They may have bruising or broken limbs as a result of falling over – most children have these kinds of accidental injuries. However, when there is further cause for concern, because the child has become either withdrawn/aggressive or other signs raise your level of concern, action does need to be taken. Other signs could include the child being less responsive than usual, flinching or even ducking away as an adult comes close. Small indicators of potential issues for a child should be noted by adults as they observe children – this will help build up a picture of what is happening in a child's life.

Sexual abuse is when an adult takes advantage of a child for their own sexual gratification. This may include inappropriate fondling.

Sexual abuse can result in damaging, long lasting effects for a child, including having difficulties in later life in forming trusting and stable personal relationships.

Emotional abuse is when there is a persistent lack of affection and physical interaction with a child, when an adult continuously fails to show love and affection, and when a child feels persistently rejected, criticised, belittled, bullied, frightened, harassed, taunted, threatening, ridiculed, ignored. This type of abuse can have an impact on the way a child feels about themselves – they may become nervous, withdrawn, lacking in confidence and self-esteem.

Neglect, or failure to thrive, is when there is a persistent or severe failure to meet a child's basis physical needs.

This may include lack of adequate food, inappropriate diet, exposing a child to cold, leaving a child unattended, inappropriate clothing, failing to attend to personal hygiene, failing to seek medical attention.

Neglect can lead to a child 'failing to thrive' and having serious health problems.

Practitioners need to be clear about recognising the signs of abuse and what they must do in order to protect the children. Safeguarding training is essential for all staff. It is crucial that everyone associated with the care of the children accept the enormous responsibility they have in keeping children safe from harm. Each member of staff must be aware of the routes of referral if abuse or poor treatment is suspected or disclosed. A 'referral' means that the setting makes contact with the Local Authority to discuss their concerns. The social worker, with their manager, will decide on next course of action if the child is regarded as being at risk of harm. In some situations, settings are advised to just monitor the situation to see if the concerns are on-going.

When making a referral, responsible adults need to consider what is most important which is, of course, the child. If an investigation does take place in the best interest of the child, a possible outcome could be that ultimately the child be removed and taken to a place of safety. What is clear is that, whenever possible, every attempt should be made to discuss concerns with the parents of the child, unless to do so may place a child at a greater risk of harm – that is,

if there were concerns that the parents may be involved in the harm of the child.

Children from all cultures and socio-economic groups can be victims of abuse – children of all ages, male and female. For some practitioners, to even believe that abuse happens in our society is hard to accept, but this is the sad reality. Practitioners need to understand the negative impact on a child's development when they have been subjected to abuse. To accept that the role of the practitioner is primarily to protect children from harm is a duty placed on all who come into contact with children and their families. Staff in all settings need to develop confidence in recognising the signs of abuse and through observation, be able to record significant changes in children's behaviour that may indicate that there is a concern to be addressed.

Each setting must have a named designated person for safeguarding – this person will be responsible for seeking advice or making a referral to safeguard a child. The document to which settings should refer for guidance is – Working Together to Safeguard Children (2013), which is Department for Education publication. The guidance became effective from 15 April 2013 and replaced Working Together to Safeguard Children (2010) and sets out how organisations and individuals should work

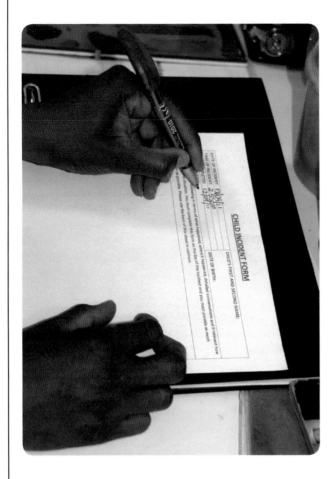

together to safeguard and promote the welfare of children. More info from the Department for Education website (www.gov.uk/dfe).

The guidance states – 'Early years providers have a duty under section 40 of the Childcare Act 2006 to comply with the welfare requirements of the Early Years Foundation Stage.

Early years providers should ensure that:

- staff complete safeguarding training that enables them to recognise signs of potential abuse and neglect; and

- they have a practitioner who is designated to take lead responsibility for safeguarding children within each early years setting and who should liaise with local statutory children's services agencies as appropriate. This lead should also complete child protection training'.

For leaders of settings

Ofsted must be informed of any allegations of abuse against a staff member, student or volunteer. This is a Statutory Framework requirement, and Ofsted will want to know what actions you have taken about the allegations, in terms of your investigation and how you have ensured that safety of the children, for example, by either suspending the person or ending their employment for gross misconduct.

Do you take up references from previous employers and explore any gaps in employment history when you appoint new staff? The references will give you an insight as to how a new member of staff has performed in their past work, although some previous employers may not give a lot of detail; they may only confirm that the person was employed by them and the dates associated to that employment. Gaps in employment history must be explored, as there may be a period of months or years when the job applicant was not employed. Circumstances such as a person being made redundant and unable to find suitable work immediately, or taking time out to raise their own child are legitimate, however, whatever the reasons, the applicant needs to clearly explain their gaps in their CV to ensure that the new employer is not concerned about whether there may be more serious reasons such as time spent in prison.

Have you made it a part of your procedures that it is an offence not to report concerns about another colleague, if children may be at risk? Do you have an open door policy that makes every member of staff feel that they can come and speak with you about any concerns they may have?

Have you made sure that every member of staff has attended a safeguarding training session and that the designated person in the setting has attended relevant training through the local authority? There are several ways in which this training can be accessed – your own local authority may offer safeguarding training, independent trainers may advertise their courses in your area, your local college may offer training for staff in your setting, and there are on-line courses that may appeal to learners. Examples of online training providers who may offer an introduction to safeguarding, refresher courses, or child protection courses are:

- Safeguarding Training (highspeedtraining.co.uk);

- Child Safeguarding Course (safeguarding.co.uk);

- Online Study Courses (OpenStudyCollege.com).

Are all your staff aware of the importance of protecting themselves against allegations of abuse? In a group setting, it is unlikely that a member of staff would be alone for more than a couple of minutes with a child, but this may happen if, for example, a child had an accident, and needed to be taken to the toilet area to be changed. The member of staff could consider:

1. Informing other staff of the situation, and state that the child is about to be taken to the toilet area to be changed.

2. If possible, remain in sight of other adults.

3. Deal as quickly as possible with the child, and then return to the main group. As far as possible, allow the child to help themselves independently.

4. Telling another member of staff what has taken place, and then advise the parent of the situation when the child is collected.

In cases of injuries, are you clear in your policy that any injuries sustained during the time you have responsibility for the children will be recorded on an accident form with signatures from witnesses and parents? An incident form would be completed when an injury to a child had been noted when the injury could not have happened in the setting, for example, a child arriving in the morning and a member of staff seeing a bruise on the child's back just after the parent had left the premises. The staff member should ask the parent about the injury, record any response i.e. their explanation, and then record any follow up dialogue with the staff member.

As part of your induction and on-going support of staff, do you ensure that all staff sign to say that they have read, understood and agree to your policies and procedures?

If an allegation of abuse is made against a member of staff, the registered person has a responsibility to take some action. An investigation will need to be carried out. This would obviously be difficult for everyone involved – especially the member of staff against whom the allegation was made. Everyone has feelings, and an investigation would be distressing.

If an allegation of abuse is made, an investigation does, regardless of feelings, need to take place – the welfare of the child is of paramount importance. Support will be needed for the member of staff, before, during and after the investigation. Your local authority support

worker is independent of your setting, and may be able to visit to offer such support. When the member of staff is interviewed, it may be agreed that he/she can ask another member of staff to be available for moral support. The outcome of the investigation will decide whether the allegation was proven, and appropriate steps will need to be taken in respect of the position of the member of staff. If the allegation is not proven, the member of staff will obviously need much support from within the setting. Confidentiality must be maintained to protect those concerned.

Clearly worded policies and procedures to protect children must be in place as well as procedures to be followed if an allegation is made against a member of staff.

So, how can you word your policy and procedure documents, so that parents fully appreciate that you are acting at all times in the best interests of the children?

On the next page, you will see examples of the wording that could be used in policy and procedure documents. Whilst parents need reassurance that you have their child's best interests at heart, they also need to know that child protection is your priority and that you are setting out how you intend to keep the children safe from harm.

Something to think about

Allegations may be made against a member of staff who has:

O   Behaved in a way that has harmed a child, or

O   Committed a criminal offence against a child, such as cruelty, or

O   Indicated that he/she may pose a risk, or potentially pose a risk, of harm to children.

Policies and Procedures – wording for your consideration

The safety and well-being of your children is our primary responsibility. If we have any concerns about your child, we will speak to you in the first instance, and hope that you will approach your child's key person if you have any concerns about your child.

This statement will tell parents that nothing matters more than the welfare of their child, and you would not hesitate to speak to the parents about any concerns you may have. This should be a reassurance to the parents.

Our staff have attended safeguarding training, and understand their responsibilities in safeguarding your children.

This statement will tell parents that the staff have the necessary knowledge to address any issues relating to the welfare of children. This too should be a reassurance to the parents, who will appreciate you being alert to these matters.

We adhere to the procedures set out by the Local Safeguarding Children's Board (LSCB). It is our duty to report any concern we may have regarding the children in our care. This is primarily to safeguard the children.

Parents will be clear about your role in safeguarding their children.

We have a designated member of staff who is our liaison person for child protection. The designated person is able to contact the Local Authority Designated Officer (LADO) for advice on child protection matters. If a member of staff has a concern about a child, the designated member of staff will be informed. A decision about how to inform you of our concerns will be made with minimum people involved. We work within the bounds of confidentiality.

Parents will be clear that you have a duty to protect children, and would contact the Local Authority LADO for advice if necessary.

Our setting requires that all members of staff share information about themselves and any close member of their family that may result in their disqualification from working with children.

Parents will appreciate that you are doing everything you can to ensure that staff are suitable to be in contact with the children in your setting.

We do not allow the personal use of mobile phones or cameras on our premises – however, we do provide a mobile phone and camera for staff, students and volunteers to use in connection with their work with the children. Images are used in accordance with the Data Protection Acts 1988 and (amended)2003, and we only use cameras where two members of staff, as a minimum, are present. The phone provided for staff is only used for work related matters.

Parents will understand that you are ensuring that the appropriate use of equipment helps you to safeguard their children.

Other policies which are relevant to safeguarding children include:

- Partnership with parents/confidentiality/late collection of children;

- Missing/lost children;

- Managing behaviour;

- Equal opportunities;

- SEN Code of Practice.

The EYFS now requires that safeguarding policies and procedures must cover the use of mobile phones and cameras in settings. (Overall Reforms to the 2012 EYFS Framework, Page 2,pt 2.) As with all written policy and procedure documents, you need to remember that they have purpose. Whether you are wording a complaint policy, a health and safety policy or a procedure for evacuation of the setting, you need to remember that the documents underpin the way in which you operate in your setting. Policy documents are about what you intend to do and procedure documents are about how you intend to bring the policy into force.

Monitoring staff practice

Managers must be satisfied that anyone employed to care for children are suitable to do so, and once employed, on-going monitoring of staff practice is necessary, so that under performance can be addressed.

Effective leadership in any setting is crucial. Monitoring of staff practice is a key responsibility of the manager. Let's look at how you can evaluate and review practice and how this can inform your plans for improvement.

Inspectors will gather evidence from their interviews with the manager and/or registered provider or their nominee, supplemented by discussion with staff and parents and, if needed, sampling of policies and procedures.

When you create an Action Plan, record:

1. How well practitioners and any trainees or students are monitored, coached, mentored and supported, and how under-performance is tackled.

2. Qualification levels and the effectiveness of a programme of professional development arising

from identified staff needs and improving relevant qualifications.

3. The deployment of staff taking account of qualifications, skills and experience.

4. The extent and range of completed training, including child protection and safeguarding training which fully meets statutory requirements, and the impact of that training in improving children's well-being.

5. The effectiveness of the staff's monitoring and revision of the educational programmes to ensure that they have sufficient depth, breadth and challenge, and reflect the needs, aptitudes and interests of children.

6. The effectiveness of the monitoring of children's progress and interventions where needed to ensure that gaps are narrowing for groups of children or individual children identified as being in need of support.

7. The effectiveness of arrangements for safeguarding, including recruitment practices and how well safe practices and a culture of safety are promoted and understood.

8. How well required policies and procedures are implemented.

9. The effectiveness of self-evaluation, including contributions from parents, carers and other stakeholders.

10. Whether well-focused improvement plans have been implemented through engagement with staff, children, parents and carers.

11. The effectiveness of arrangements for sharing information and working in partnership with other providers, schools and professionals in order to identify all children's needs and help them to make good progress.

As part of your Action Plan, evaluate the effectiveness of what you have in place. In this way, you can show how, as an on-going process, you are looking to make improvements.

How well are staff and any trainees or students monitored, coached, mentored and supported, and how is under-performance tackled?

From the start, an induction package will provide any new member of staff, trainee/student/young person on their work experience week with comprehensive information about the setting, including policies, procedures, dress code and staff behaviour/responsibilities.

The pack should not be just handed over, but be carefully explained. Do you have a designated person who supports

Something to think about

○ Photos should only be taken of children whose parents have given prior written permission for this to happen.

○ The circumstances of when photos can be taken and used should be made quite clear to both parents and staff. For example, a parent may agree to having a photo of their child taken as part of their progress records but not for general use in a prospectus, display or for a newspaper report.

○ Staff should not take photos on their own cameras or phones.

○ Parents need to consult with the management if they wish to take photos of activities their child takes part in – example, performances.

○ Photos, if permitted, should be for personal use only. Under no circumstances must any photo be posted on a social networking site.

○ Mobile phones should not be used by staff during sessions. Their main priority is the care and wellbeing of the children.

○ Staff should be supervising the children at all times. However, mobile phones are useful when taking children on outings and the setting should have a clear policy on this.

○ Parents should be made aware that the general use of mobile phones is not acceptable in the setting.

CASE STUDY: INAPPROPRIATE USE OF MOBILE PHONES
Source – Plymouth Safeguarding Children's Board

Background

A nursery nurse had taken indecent photographs of young children at the Plymouth nursery where she was employed.

When this became public knowledge, there was an understandable reaction within the early years sector and beyond – naturally, parents everywhere had thoughts about the settings where they had placed their children – how could they get reassurance that their children were safe? Staff in settings had thoughts about how they could provide this reassurance to parents as they reviewed their own procedures.

Plymouth Council launched a serious case review and their report was published on 4 November 2010.

Plymouth Serious Case Review

'The report says that from staff interviews and discussions with parents, as well as a review of the records, it was apparent that the nursery did not provide a safe, positive environment for children in its care. It says: "This would indicate that either the individual inspections were not rigorous enough, or the framework for inspection is not adequate."

The environment enabled a culture to develop in which staff did not feel able to challenge some inappropriate behaviour displayed by the nursery nurse. Staff working at the nursery became increasingly uncomfortable and worried about her behaviour but felt they had nowhere to go with these feelings.

There appears to have been a complete lack of recognition of the seriousness of the boundary violation and a culture in which explicit sexual references about adults in conversation were the norm. (*Inappropriate conversations between adults in settings must be avoided at all times due to the effect on the children.*)

What could we learn from this review?

The report concluded that while ultimate responsibility for the abuse rested with the nursery nurse and that no "professional could have reasonably predicted that she might be a risk to children", there were several failings in nursery's management, recruitment, staff reporting and other arrangements, which had "provided an ideal environment" for her to abuse.

So, with the report concluding that the nursery provided an ideal environment within which the nursery nurse could abuse, what lessons could be learned? The serious case review report details a number of lessons learned, which include:

O   The important role the Early Years Service can play in identifying poor practice within nursery settings. The report says: "There is much good practice by the Early Years Service, who made strenuous efforts to work with the nursery to improve the experience of children attending."

O   The danger of mobile phones within day care settings. The report says: "Whilst stopping staff carrying mobile phones is an important preventative measure and will mean that images cannot easily be transmitted electronically; this alone will not prevent abuse taking place."

O   An urgent need to develop effective staff supervision within early years settings.

O   The separation of the regulator (Ofsted) from Early Years Services means the communications pathway is not flexible enough to allow sharing of information which could inform a judgement about good practice.

O   Staff did not recognise the escalation of the nursery nurse's sexualised behaviour as a warning sign and there is an urgent need for staff working in early years settings to receive training to help recognise potential signs of abuse and become confident in responding to a fellow staff member's behaviour.

The conclusion of the report is that while there were a number of factors that came together to support a culture where abuse was possible and a number of lessons to be learned, "ultimate responsibility for the abuse must rest with the nursery nurse".

The review makes a series of key recommendations including national recommendations. They are:

O   Clear communications mechanisms should be set up between Ofsted and early years advisory teams to ensure local intelligence informs the nursery inspection process.

O   The Early Years Foundation Stage safeguarding requirements should be reviewed and strengthened in order to identify the characteristics of unsafe organisations. Further guidance should be issued to early years Ofsted inspectors to help them identify where these characteristics may exist. This should include safer recruitment procedures.

O The Early Years Foundation Stage should set out specific requirements for child protection training which considers sexual abuse and the recognition of abuse within the workplace.

O Government should review and consider changing the status of day care settings operating as unincorporated bodies to ensure that governance and accountability arrangements are fit for purpose and are sufficiently clear to enable parents and professionals to raise concerns and challenge poor practice.

new people in the setting and who is the key person to go to if they have any concerns?

Every member of staff should have supervision meetings with a senior member of staff or manager, depending on the size of the setting. It is always straightforward when a manager can just 'tick the boxes' to show that a member of staff is performing well and always looking to improve their practice. Under performance must be addressed – however difficult the conversation. Best practice would be a clear system of 1:1 meetings and appraisals for all staff that are consistent across the setting.

Every member of staff needs to understand why a written system of supervision and appraisal is in place:

1. Both the manager and supervisee need a record of what was discussed and agreed.

2. Both the manager and supervisee need to be clear about any matters of disagreement.

3. For the process to show consistency in supervision for all staff.

At the end of the supervision meeting, which would normally take about 30 minutes, both manager and supervisee would sign to agree the actions identified, and to agree the accuracy of the discussions that have taken place. Each keep a copy – the manager's copy must be kept securely in the Supervision and Appraisal File, which forms a part of the Leadership and Support File that needs to be in place for Ofsted. Staff under performance, which can have an adverse effect on children, must be discussed and recorded.

It is important to all concerned that the supervisee is comfortable in discussing all aspects of their work. To provide the supervisee with reassurance, the manager should confirm

that the supervision and appraisals record will be accessible to us both parties any time. The supervisee needs to be aware that, although these are confidential documents, they are also organisational documents which do not belong solely to the manager and supervisee.

As such, the supervision and appraisal record is neither secret nor private.

The following circumstances may arise, when the records may be shared with others:

● Auditing;

● Grievance;

● Discipline;

● Internal/external inquiry;

● Complaints.

An effective system of supervision and appraisal, alongside monitoring of staff practice, will enable leaders to support staff in keeping all children safe.

Example Appraisal Process (a guide to a system of recording)

APPRAISAL PROCESS   PRIVATE AND CONFIDENTIAL

Employee Name: Appraiser Name:

Appraisal Meeting Date: Appraisal period:

Job Description/Responsibilities:

IMPORTANT: Part A of this form will be completed by the employee and handed in to the appraiser (Manager) one week before the arranged meeting date. Part B will be completed by the appraiser (Manager) prior to the appraisal meeting. Part C will be left blank and will be completed by the appraiser (Manager) during the meeting.

PART A: TO BE COMPLETED BY THE EMPLOYEE

What have you achieved in your key area of work during the appraisal period?

What do you consider to be your key strengths?

Does your job description accurately reflect your current duties and if not please comment here.

What skills/area of work do you feel you need to improve the most?

Which parts of your job do you like the most?

Are there any aspects of your job that you don't enjoy? Please comment here.

What are your personal work goals for the next year?

Do you feel there is anything that I could do to help you meet you goals and perform more effectively?

Please comment on any areas/issues that have not been addressed?

Example Appraisal Process continued (a guide to a system of recording)

PART B: TO BE COMPLETED BY THE APPRAISER (MANAGER) PRIOR TO THE MEETING

What has the appraisee achieved in their key area of work during the appraisal period?

What are their key strengths?

Are there areas they can improve upon?

What goals would you like to see achieved in this next period?

Does the appraisee routinely undertake any duties outside of their job description?

PART C: TO BE COMPLETED BY THE APPRAISER (MANAGER) DURING THE MEETING

After reviewing and discussing the employee's comments to **PART A** and the appraiser's comments to **PART B**, the appraiser should use **PART C** to record their agreed comments and future training/targets agreed with the employee during the meeting. This meeting may take up to one hour.

What has been agreed as key strengths and achievements over this last period?

What has been agreed as areas for improvement?

How is this being supported?

General comments (including actions to be taken forward with review of job description). Listed here will be any training needs or targets set for the employee: If applicable, has the appraisee successfully completed their probationary period? If no, please add comments as to why not.

Section 2:
Discovering boundaries

For some children, learning right from wrong, and accepting that boundaries are necessary for us all to enjoy our time together, is hard! This may be because there have been no boundaries set at home – boundaries that relate to behaviour need to be reinforced within the setting for all children.

In this section we will look at the environment and the impact on the children's development when environmental factors are given a priority in the setting.

What is meant by the term 'a safe environment'? Whilst the role of the practitioner is to keep children safe as they play and explore, there are three areas of the environment we need to explore:

The emotional environment
The emotional environment is created by all the people in the setting, but adults have to ensure that it is warm and accepting of everyone. Adults need to empathise with children and support their emotions. When children feel confident in the environment they are willing to try things out, knowing that effort is valued. When children know that their

feelings are accepted they learn to express them, confident that adults will help them with how they are feeling.

The indoor environment
The indoor environment provides a safe, secure yet challenging space for children. For some children, the indoor environment is like a second home, providing a place for activity, rest, eating and sleeping. The indoor environment has resources which are age and stage appropriate, well maintained and accessible for all children. Indoor spaces are planned so that they can be used flexibly and an appropriate range of activities are provided.

The outdoor environment
Being outdoors has a positive impact on children's sense of well being and helps in all aspects of children's development. Being outdoors offers opportunities for doing things in different ways and on different scales than when indoors. It gives children direct contact with the weather, seasons and the natural world. Outdoor environments offer children freedom to explore, use their senses, and be physically active too.

'Keeping children safe' is about environmental considerations as well as about harm in terms of abuse. Adults working in the setting play a key role in ensuring the safety of the children. It is therefore important that all staff have been through a thorough and appropriate recruitment and vetting procedure.

The Government's statutory guidance 'Working Together to Safeguard the Children' emphasises that safe recruitment is essential to prevent unsuitable people gaining access to and posing a risk to children.

So what recruiting and vetting procedures are in place in your setting?

Once recruited, staff should be made familiar with all the policies and procedures of the setting as part of their induction and ongoing training. However, if temporary or agency staff are used to cover a shortfall in personnel, it is essential that they are made aware of the procedures of the setting, as these will differ from place to place.

Adults need to anticipate and assess the risks in all areas to minimise the possibility of children coming to harm. Children need to rely on 'their adults' for the security of the building and the outside areas.

Think about who has access to the building and area. What systems are in place to ensure the safe arrival and departure of the children? Does your setting meet in a shared building, for example, do other organisations use rooms or areas in the same premises? This may happen in community halls. If so, what are the possible risks to the children?

All staff need to be vigilant around drop off and collection times and when visitors come and go, whether they are expected, unexpected, delivering or on site to do a job of work. Parents/carers arriving with or collecting children should be greeted by a member of staff and the children logged in and registered or recorded as leaving. Some settings have a coded or other electronic system for entry but staff and parents/carers should be aware of the possibility of unauthorised persons entering the building. Is that person for whom a helpful parent is holding the door open really a new parent? It is essential to make sure that parents do not hold open doors for other people or if there is a coded entry system that the codes are not shared with others.

Visitors

During the day, how does your setting deal with visitors, deliveries and tradesmen? Not everyone will have an appointment but all should be asked for identification, the reason for their visit and logged into the visitor's record. Personnel from your Head Office, whom you may know,

When recruiting new staff think about:

O Legal requirements, as set out in the revised EYFS (2014)

O Job description and person specification

O Interview process with regard to equality of opportunity and with regard to an applicant's C.V.

O Two references; one should be from the candidate's last employer

O Appropriate employment checks including the right of the individual to work in the United Kingdom. The booklet 'Safer Recruitment: Confirming an Individual's Eligibility or 'Right to Work' in the UK' gives guidance on the documents that can be used to help check this. Passports are one way of checking identification.

O Evidence of Qualifications. Staff who have trained overseas may not count as qualified staff unless their qualifications are recognised by Ofsted. The Department for Education has indicated that it will accept the judgement of the National Academic Recognition Centre, (NARIC) on whether overseas qualifications are equivalent to those available in the UK. UK NARIC works on behalf of the UK Government to provide a range of advisory services which compare international qualifications.

O Candidates should be made aware that they will need to be vetted through the Disclosure and Barring Service (DBS) and that enhanced checks will be taken up.

O The Statutory Framework for the EYFS states that: 'Providers must tell staff that they are expected to disclose any convictions, cautions, court orders, reprimands and warnings which may affect their suitability to work with children (whether received before or during their employment at the setting.) (3.11)

O Candidates need to be aware that, whilst there is not a specific requirement for staff to speak English, the Statutory Framework for EYFS (3.25) states 'Providers must ensure that staff have sufficient understanding and use of English to ensure the well-being of children in their care. For example, settings must be in a position to keep records in English, to liaise with other agencies in English, to summon emergency help, and to understand instructions such as those for the safety of medicines or food hygiene.' Also, providers need to consider the impact on the safety of the children if they cannot understand what the staff are saying.

CASE STUDY: A MISSING CHILD

Consider the following report in the press of a child leaving a nursery unobserved: *'CCTV footage shows the child slipped out during a busy lunch period when staff and parents were holding the doors open." It appears that "the child got out because staff and parents were holding the door open for "multiple intervals".The setting 'apologised for what happened and said it had "drawn up a rigorous action plan designed to address issues raised".'* (Source: web page of Hull Daily Mail November 8th 2013 www.hulldailymail.co.uk)

What policies and procedures are in place at your setting which would prevent such an incident occurring? Should you review those you have in place after reading about this incident?

Is there a clear arrival and collection policy in place?

Something to think about

○ Open doors are very inviting to children who are curious about the world around them. Children have very little idea of the danger which may be outside.

○ Do you know who is collecting the child? What steps should you take if someone else turns up to collect the child? Think about what you need to do. You would not allow a child to leave with someone that you are unaware of, so it may be that you can call the parent for confirmation of who they have asked to collect their child. This would need to be recorded and, for future reference, you could agree with the parent that they will advise you, in writing, of any changes to the collection times or person due to arrive to collect their child.

○ Normally, you would not deny either parent access to their child, but there may be a court order in place making clear the name of any person who may not collect a child. You may need a copy of the court order to enable you to enforce this.

○ What happens if a child is not collected? You should have a procedure on this. If neither parent can be contacted, and the emergency named person is not contactable either you will need to call your local social services so that the child can be taken to a safe location, such as to a close family member until the parents can be located.

○ Are contact numbers for parents/carers up to date?

officials from the Local Authority, and any inspectors working for Ofsted should be logged in and out.

Issue them with a visitors badge and where applicable record the registration number of their vehicle. Depending on their business within the setting, is there a member of staff available to be with them? Staff too should record their arrival and departure and any other times when they leave the setting. This is important not only for fire/evacuation purposes but for management to maintain correct staff/child ratios.

Often visitors are advised of what they should do in the case of having to evacuate from the setting but are they made aware of the security aspects?

Consider this situation:

'A two-year-old girl left a nursery unnoticed and walked half a mile home on her own. The girl left the nursery at about 13:00 and arrived home shortly after, saying: "Mummy, I'm home". Police said a workman is believed to have left a door at the nursery open.' (Source: BBC on line 5 September 2013).

Thankfully, these incidents do not occur frequently. However, there are instances where even the most vigilant

Something to think about

O Put children's needs first at all times.

O The primary role of the practitioner is to keep each child safe.

O Aim to keep children safe by adopting the highest possible standards and taking all reasonable steps to protect children from harm.

O Develop trusting relationships with children, so that they know you will respond to them – they will be listened to and believed. For some children, to tell an adult about something that is happening to them is a major step; they may be frightened about what may happen next, they may have been threatened about disclosing the situation, and they may be fearful that the adult will not believe them. It is therefore crucial that the adult hearing what the child has to say will be supportive and give the child all the time they need to talk about their situation.

of staff are fallible. Articles in the press have cited cases where mistakes have been made by adults.

An example of this was about a grandfather who took his granddaughter to the wrong nursery school. As her older sister attended the school, he did not realise that the two year old attended a different nursery, and not the one attached to the school. A member of staff, covering for a colleague, accepted the child. When the mistake was realised, staff tried to contact the grandparent but were not successful and subsequently called the police. At the end of the afternoon the child was reunited with her mother.

This helps to highlight the importance of the key worker system and the overall knowledge that the staff should have of the children in their care.

By establishing and developing positive relationships with the children and their parents, the key worker can help the child to feel safe, develop confidence and to feel secure within the environment. Key workers are important in helping children to become familiar with the setting. By building up a relationship of trust they can identify any changes in behaviour which may indicate that the child is having problems. They provide consistent boundaries and will monitor the progress of the child, particularly their emotional and developmental needs through observation, assessment and record keeping.

Children are naturally curious and enjoy exploring, investigating and discovering – that is, learning about the

CASE STUDY: A CHILD'S AWARENESS OF DANGER

Woodlands Day Nursery, West Berkshire

'Finding a balance or happy medium between being aware of the dangers that children in our care may be faced with and being over protective of them because of the fear of these dangers becoming a reality, is always a difficult balance to achieve, however we feel it is vital if we are to support children in their development. Firstly it is of the upmost importance for us to know what dangers the children may be faced with, this includes not only the daily health and safety issues that can arise within the nursery setting but also dangers that the children may be faced with outside the setting. With relation to safe guarding it is important to aim to achieve the balance between providing children with the knowledge of what is a 'danger' to them and how to react when faced with these and not scaring children with the 'stranger danger' talk. In a recent study we found it interesting to see that when asked to pick out a picture of a 'stranger' most children picked the same photo, of a man with facial hair and therefore did not see that others such as a woman or another child could also be a 'stranger' to them. We believe that it is important through topics such as 'people who help us' and through discussions using events in children's books such as a teddy getting lost, to provide children with the knowledge of what they should do if faced with a situation that makes them feel 'sad' or 'scared' and who they can speak to. As children grow up they will often go through phases where they don't recognise 'acceptable' behaviour for example they will often go through a phase where they will kiss all their friends or will not recognise situation when lack of clothing is not appropriate i.e. walking out of the toilet before getting fully dressed. Through these phases it is important to remind the children of the boundaries, talking about who we save our kisses for and reminding them about clothing etc. It is important to try and provide children with the knowledge of what is acceptable and who is a 'safe' person that they can speak to if they need to'.

When it comes to recognising dangers within the environment, although some dangers need to be taught to the children to avoid harm, other activities will allow children to recognise and within reason experience the danger themselves. Children need to be allowed to gain personal experience of what the dangers are so that they can know how to avoid them in the future'. Remember to think about each child individually. Some children will recognise danger more easily than others. Some children do not see danger at all.

way, children can come to understand that we can all take some responsibility in keeping our play areas safe.

Risk assessing all areas of your setting

The Health and Safety Executive (HSE) have produced, on behalf of the Government, a leaflet entitled **'5 Steps to Risk Assessment'**. It sets out how to assess the risks in your workplace.

- 'Step 1. Identify the hazards.'
  Identify any possible hazards by risk assessing all areas both inside and out. (You could involve older children by asking them to let adults know if they find anything that is broken.)

- 'Step 2. Decide who might be harmed and how.'
  What could happen and what actions should be taken to prevent or minimise this risk?

- 'Step 3. Evaluate the risks and decide on precautions.'
  It may be that there are already preventative measures and policies and procedures in place. But is everyone aware of these measures?

- 'Step 4. Record your findings and implement them.'
  Any concerns should be reported to managers so that action can be taken. Failure to do so, could result in an accident.

- 'Step 5. Review your assessment and update if necessary.'
  This is an opportunity for staff to evaluate the process and determine how effective the assessments are.

Assessing the risks: indoors

If your setting operates in a building shared with other users, it is important to acknowledge the possible problems posed by other equipment or areas not usually used with the children, for example: adult sized chairs stacked at the back of the hall; sports equipment; staging etc. Where practical, discuss with the owners and other users as sometimes they can be unaware of the fact that items left out can pose a risk to young children. Ensure that you and the rest of the staff team take steps to minimise any possible risks from these potential hazards.

When carrying out your own risk assessments, you need to remember that because children are smaller than adults, they will see things from a different height. It is worth looking at the environment from the child's perspective. A display which is aesthetically pleasing for the adults and showcases the children's work may not be at a height for

world around them. However, as young children do not understand danger, adults should make the environment, both inside and outside as safe as possible for them. Risk assessments for all areas of the setting are important and form the basis of your Self-Evaluation Form (SEF) and provide evidence of good management. The Statutory Framework for Early Years Foundation Stage is specific about this. 'Providers must have a clear and well-understood policy and procedures for assessing any risks to children's safety and review risk assessments regularly.'

Risk assessments should identify aspects of the environment that need to be checked on a regular basis, when and by whom those aspects will be checked, and how the risk will be removed or minimised.

However, even though it can involve more paperwork, written risk assessments or check lists to be used by staff daily are an additional safeguard to the safety of children. All staff will have the same base to work from. These should not be just 'pieces of paper' or a computer file but should be working documents updated regularly. Across the setting, all staff should be responsible for daily checks. You could consider involving older children in looking at risks to safe play. For example, when the children are due to go outside, you could suggest that if they find anything that is broken, they could find an adult who can deal with it. In this

Keeping Safe

the children to appreciate as well. Look at everything from a child's perspective as well as an adult perspective. Think about the children within each room or area. Bear in mind their ages, stage of development and what they might be likely to do in terms of their explorations.

When looking at the areas where the children are mainly cared for, assess the rooms when unoccupied as well as when the children are in the room. A well laid out room when empty may not be as safe and practical when little people are in and using the equipment and playthings provided. For example there may need to be more space between furniture and equipment when children are using them.

Start at the front door. Possible problems regarding access and children leaving unnoticed have already been explored.

Beyond the security of the entrance door, think about the following:

- Entrance area. Think about the information that is displayed there for adults. Sometimes there can be too much on show which results in essential information being overlooked by parents and visitors. Information about the settings certificate of registration, insurance, evacuation procedures and safety should be prominent;

- Is the entrance hall and any corridors kept clear of any obstacles such as excess furniture, equipment, buggies and car seats?

- Displays should be safe and secure and not liable to fall or able to be pulled down by the children. This is important throughout all the rooms, not just the entrance hall. Seasonal items such as Christmas trees and decorations should be located away from the main walkways;

- Are fire exits easily identified and not obstructed? Are fire doors kept closed and not propped open for convenience?

- Are stairs safe? Are the surfaces of the steps showing signs of wear and tear? What is located at the top and bottom of these, for example doors? Are safety gates in use? Are the handrails at a child's height?

- Are there any areas such as the kitchen and the office where children could go unsupervised? How can you make these inaccessible for children?

- Play rooms – are floors clear of clutter and toys? Is the flooring safe and suitable for the age and stage of the children using the area? Is there sufficient room for the children to move safely between activities?

- Can the children move around freely? Is there enough room for all children to sit, for example, on the floor when listening to a story or at tables when having lunch?

- The majority of windows today are fitted with safety glass but it is worth checking. Are windows secured to prevent children from climbing out, that is, fixed so that they will only open an inch or so? If locked with a key, are the keys kept easily accessible in the case of an emergency but out of the reach of the children? Make sure that there is not any furniture beneath windows which children could climb up on to reach the windows;

- Are there blinds at the windows where cords could be a hazard? Are curtains/blinds in place to minimise the effects of glare from the sun and to darken areas which are used for sleeping/resting?

- Doors. Are these self closing? Is there a possibility of children catching their fingers in the door? If there are no vision panels in the internal doors, are adults vigilant to ensure that there are no children near the door when anyone comes in or leaves? Areas around doorways should be kept clear of any toys, furniture and equipment;

- Bathroom areas. If your setting does not meet in a purpose built building, there are considerations – if the toilets are not child sized, steps and child sized toilet seats may be needed, as well as potties. These should be kept scrupulously clean and good practice would be for each child to have his/her own labelled potty. Toilet brushes should be inaccessible to children and consideration should be given to items such as toilet blocks being removed. Children should not be able to lock themselves into a toilet. If the toilet doors cannot be opened from the outside by an adult, 'over the door' stops or jammers should be used. Are flannels available for the children? How do you ensure that children do not use other children's flannels?

- Children love to play with water and often will spend a long time 'washing their hands'. What products are in use for the children to use? What are you providing for children to dry their hands with? Some children are not happy to use hand drying machines and this can cause distress. Are toothbrushes and toothpaste available for the children to use after meals? Toothbrushes should be labelled and parents advised of the tooth paste used so that they can check the contents in case of allergies;

- Changing mats should be kept scrupulously clean and disinfected after every use. Don't forget to look underneath the mat when cleaning! If the change area is

kept clean, and the adults are particular about hygiene matters, there will be less risk of germs spreading.

Furniture, toys and equipment

Furniture and fittings should be fit for purpose and age and stage appropriate. Younger children may use tables and chairs to pull themselves up or as aids to balancing and walking. Children should not be encouraged to climb on tables.

Toys and equipment should be clean and in good condition. Check that there are no loose pieces.

Make sure that children have age and stage appropriate toys. Young children tend to put everything in their mouths, so do not allow, especially small babies, to play with items with small parts which could pose a choking problem. Use a choke hazard testing tube if you are uncertain. These tubes can be purchased from toy shops or through authorised sellers on the internet. They can be used to test not just toys but other objects to determine whether they should be kept away from the youngest children in your setting. Play items which are put in mouths by the children should be washed daily to prevent any chance of cross infection.

- Never let children of any age play with uninflated or broken balloons because of the choking danger;

- Toys with batteries: Staff should make sure batteries are secure within the item so that children cannot remove them.

High chairs, prams, pushchairs must be well maintained and checked daily before use. Restraints such as harnesses and reins should be complete and clean. High chairs and low feeding chairs need to be sanitised thoroughly after each use. Think about where older children could have put their hands on chairs – what about the undersides of these and of tables?

Some children may need specialist equipment such as wheelchairs and it is important that there is sufficient space for these when in use or when stored.

Children benefit from a wide range of different experiences. Adults should ensure that equipment is appropriate and of good quality. Out of necessity, items such as gardening tools, tools for woodworking, knives and scissors need to be sharp. The children need to be supervised at all times and shown how to use these safely and correctly.

Sleeping areas

Sleeping arrangements differ from setting to setting. However, the following points apply to all settings:

- Children should not, under any circumstances, share bedding. Age appropriate bedding should be used. Mattresses and sleep mats should be routinely cleaned after use. Both these measures help to prevent cross contamination;

- It is good practice for the setting to advise parents of the products it uses to launder items in case of a child having allergies;

- When sleeping mats are used there should be enough room for an adult to walk easily between the mats in case a child needs some attention. Also if the mats are touching, the children could also touch each other thereby disturbing others;

- Mats, etc. should be stored away after use where children cannot access them.

Kitchen

There are many hazards in the kitchen such as cookers, fridges, freezers, kettles, toasters, dish washers, sharp knives etc. Children should not be allowed in the kitchen at any time unless strictly supervised by an adult. If children are taken into the kitchen area for cooking activities as there is no other area available, the dangers and hazards should be assessed by the adults before hand and every effort made to ensure safety. Good hygiene practices need to be observed, for example good hand washing to prevent germs and cross-contamination.

Storage areas

Throughout the setting there should be storage space for all types of items. Depending on the premises, storage will vary from walk-in areas, large cupboards, open shelving, book cases and sheds. It is worth doing a review of what your setting has to offer in terms of storage. It may be that

you could utilise the spaces more effectively for the benefit of all.

- Indoors, there should be separate space for storing toys and play materials, bedding, towels, nappies etc.;

- Cleaning equipment which is used in the playrooms, such as dustpans and brushes, brooms, mops and buckets should be appropriately stored away from areas the children use. It is tempting to place these in bathroom areas but not good practice;

- In all areas there should be allocated space for each child's personal items, for example, coats, outdoor shoes etc. For older children these should be at a height where they can access these for themselves, so promoting independence;

- Consider where parents can store their buggies and car seats if they need to leave these with you;

- Outdoors – storage areas are usually sheds. These should be kept locked or secured so that the children cannot get into these;

- Cleaning materials should be stored well out of the reach of the children, preferably in a cupboard fitted

---

Something to think about

O Are your cupboards crammed with items that are not likely to be used again? This may be an opportunity to sort through what is no longer needed.

O Do you provide storage space for staff belongings? For example, lockable cupboards.

O Do you encourage children to return items to shelves or drawers, that they have finished using?

---

with childproof catches. Children enjoy playing with sprays and will not realise that those used for cleaning are not safe as the sprays which they use in water play;

- Cleaning products should be kept in the original containers and clearly labelled.

All settings need to be aware of COSHH. This stands for Control of Substances Hazardous to Health Regulations 2002. It is the law that requires employers to control substances that are hazardous to health. Further information can be obtained from the Health and Safety Executive (HSE). Basically, a provider can prevent or reduce workers exposure to hazardous substances by:

- finding out what the health hazards are;

- deciding how to prevent harm to health (risk assessment);

- providing control measures to reduce harm to health and making sure that they are used.

- providing information, instruction and training for employees and others;

- providing monitoring and health surveillance in appropriate cases;

- planning for emergencies.

Sometimes substances are easily recognised as harmful. However common substances such as paint, bleach or dust from natural materials are also harmful.

Electrical items

- The Health & Safety at Work Act (1974) and 'The Electricity at Work Regulations place a legal responsibility on employers, employees and self-employed persons to comply with the provisions of the regulations and take reasonably practicable steps to ensure that no danger results from the use of such equipment.' This means that items should be inspected frequently to ensure that they are in a safe condition. PAT testing or portable appliance testing is an important part of any health and safety policy. Remember:

- Turn all electrical equipment off after use;

- Make sure that there are no trailing leads;

- Items in play rooms such as free standing fans in hot weather should be sited away from the children and staff should ensure that children cannot get near these;

- Electric powered extractor fans in toilet, bathroom areas should have leads shortened so that only adults can reach these;

- Any sockets that are not in use should have safety covers fitted;

- Radiators should be regulated so that they do not get too hot. If necessary fit radiator covers;

- Televisions and other electrical appliances such as DVD and CD players should be kept out of reach of the children.

Fire safety

All fire fighting equipment should be tested annually and the dates when this is carried out recorded for inspection by the Fire Officer. The fire equipment should include fire extinguishers and fire blankets. Smoke and carbon monoxide detectors should be regularly checked.

Children should be made aware but not alarmed by the fact that sometimes they need to leave the premises when they

A **HAZARD** is something a child does not see.

A **RISK** is a challenge a child **can** see, and chooses to undertake or not.

Eliminating risk leads to a child's inability to assess danger.

The emergency alarm has been sounded for a practice drill and as room leader it is your responsibility to ensure the safe evacuation of your area. Once outside, you check the register and find that a child who is marked in as attending that day has not come out with the group. What should you do?

You may:

O Check with other staff members if they have seen the child.

O Check with other room leaders that the child has not joined their group.

O Initiate a search of the area where the child should have been.

O If this is not successful, the person in charge should put into place a full scale search both inside and outside of the setting.

Other considerations:

O Sufficient staff should remain to care for the other children but any other staff may assist with looking for the missing child.

O The parents/carers of the child should be contacted and the police called.

O The Police will then take over.

O The incident should be recorded and OFSTED informed.

O Draw up a missing child policy and procedure or if there is one already in place, review and if needed, rewrite.

hear a bell or alarm. They need to know what is expected of them, such as listening to instructions, walking up and down stairs in a safe way and listening when their name is called, if applicable, once outside.

Evacuation drills should be practised regularly so that the children do not become distressed or frightened. Some settings make use of items such as ropes which the children hold onto 'making a train' so that the children file out in an ordered way.

It is worth considering having time to discuss fire drills with the children, reading relevant stories and have role playing areas such as the fire station.

Keep a record of when drills take place and try to practice at different times of the day. Emergencies won't wait for it to be fine and sunny outside or for a child to finish his or her painting! Ideally, only the person in charge should know when the 'emergency is going to happen' as this is a way of determining how quickly and effectively the adults and children have exited the building.

Fire and evacuation procedures

Clear written instructions for evacuation should be placed in all rooms. These should:

● State what action the staff should take if they discover the need for evacuation, either through fire or other emergency such as raising the alarm or reacting to it;

● Identify the nearest escape route and if possible an alternative in case the first route is inaccessible;

● State clearly the assembly point or designated place of safety;

● Show the location of the nearest telephone in case needed.

In addition:

- A designated member of staff should take charge of calling the Fire Service or other services for example, the gas board;

- Staff should ensure that they take the room register with them when leaving the premises, so that a check can be made to ensure that everyone is accounted for;

- A member of staff should be designated to check each area such as toilets to see that there is no one left inside the building;

- Parents should be made aware that in the case of an emergency they should collect their child from the designated assembly point and not try to enter the building, for their own safety.

Emergencies and First Aid

Emergencies can happen at any time. Parents should give written permission for the setting to seek emergency medical help and a form drawn up for each child authorising this. This is important for all children but especially crucial for children who may have an allergy – for example, to peanuts.

- Think about what could constitute an emergency. Are all staff aware of the types of accidents and what action should be taken?

- Think about when an ambulance needs to be called;

- Is your settings policy clear?

- Are the procedures in place detailed enough for all adults to understand, not just the management?

- Are staff familiar with 'The Reporting of Injuries, Diseases and Dangerous Occurrences Regulations 2013,' (RIDDOR) and when it should be implemented? This regulates the statutory obligation to report deaths, injuries, diseases and dangerous occurrences that take place at work or in connection with work. An example of a dangerous occurrence could be 'the accidental release of any substance which could cause injury to any person.' (www.hse.gov.uk/riddor).

As with the recording of any possible signs and indicators of abuse outlined in Section 1 of this book, settings should have records of any accidents, the action taken and any treatment given or advice sought which should be counter signed by the parent or carer. Even seemingly insignificant incidents such as a small cut or a bumped head should be recorded. These records should be confidential but are also a useful tool for management when reviewing safety within the nursery as if several accidents/incidents of a similar nature have occurred in the same area or at much the same time, there may be a need to look at what is happening and possible causes. If necessary, routines and practice should be changed.

The Statutory Framework for the EYFS says 'Providers must ensure there is a first aid box accessible at all times with appropriate content for use with children.' (3.48) and 'At least one person who has a current paediatric first aid certificate must be on the premises at all times when children are present, and must accompany children on outings.' (3.24)

However, good practice would be that each play room should have a first aid box easily accessible and that more than one trained first aider is on hand within the setting.

Any medication which a child may need, should be located in the area where the child is based, for example, a child with a known peanut allergy should have their EpiPen nearby in case of an anaphylactic shock. All adults need to know where the medication is, and it should be readily accessible, but out of reach of the children, preferably in a lockable medicine cabinet. If the medicine needs to be kept refrigerated, reminders should be recorded as to when a dose is needed. In the Statutory Framework for the EYFS, parents must give

O Although it is fun and of great interest to most children to have pets or visiting animals in the setting, it is important to remember that there are risks of infection associated with animals.

O Hand washing is crucial in helping in controlling the spread of infection.

O Children should always wash their hands before meals, after using the toilet as well as after they have handled animals.

O If an adult or a child has a cut, a waterproof dressing is necessary to cover the cut to prevent infection.

written permission for any medicine to administered and that 'providers must keep a written record each time a medicine is administered to a child, and inform the child's parent and/or carers on the same day, or as soon as reasonably practicable.'(3.44)

For more information, useful contacts are:

- Royal Society for the Prevention of Accidents (RoSPA) (www.rospa.com);

- Child Accident Prevention Trust (CAPT) (www.capt.org.uk);

- British Red Cross (www.redcross.org.uk);

- St John Ambulance (www.sja.org.uk).

Pets

Some settings keep pets for the children to see and handle. Many young children enjoy interacting with animals but some are wary. Others may not like the pets due to past experiences. Caring for the pets teaches the children responsibility for other creatures and not just themselves.

- Parents need to be made aware that the setting has pets and what they are;

- Some children have allergies to feathers and fur so animals with these could pose a danger to them;

- Children need to be shown how to handle pets in the correct way. They should only do so under direct supervision of an adult. Children need to be reminded that pets are not toys and it is possible to hurt them

unintentionally. Even the most placid animal can turn and bite if handled inappropriately;

- The children should be made aware of the rules for looking after animals, feeding them and cleaning out their homes. They should be made aware of the importance of washing hands after handling a pet or cleaning out their cage;

- If children are taken out on farm visits or have a farm brought to the setting, staff should remember that the children will not have interacted with these particular animals before. An example of this could be horses. They can easily become upset by children shouting and screaming. The children should be reminded not to be behind a horse as it may kick out. Inevitably the children will want to feed and stroke them so it is important to demonstrate how to stroke one way and to hold the food on the palm of a flat hand to ensure that little fingers do not get chewed;

- Suitable pets include fish that require little attention but must be housed in a commercial aquarium which conforms to the safety standards. Small mammals such as gerbils or guinea pigs can be kept in cages and rabbits can be kept in hutches. With careful and repeated handling, all small mammals can become tame but may scratch if frightened;

- Some children will enjoy interacting with bugs and insects such as snails, beetles and millipedes. Again, children will need to be shown how to handle these safely and correctly.

Assessing the risks: outdoors

The EYFS emphasises the importance of high quality outdoor experiences and highlighted is the importance of free flow play.

Young children should be outdoors as much as indoors and need a well-designed, well organised integrated indoor-outdoor environment, preferably with indoors and outdoors available simultaneously.

Although young children need to be able to take acceptable levels of risk in their play in order to learn and develop, adults have a duty to ensure that the environment is safe.

Is the outdoor area checked for hazards prior to the children using the area? Who is responsible for this?

Are the outside gates and perimeter fences intact and secure? Are there any areas where a child might get through while unobserved?

Are there any areas where 'strangers' can observe or come into contact with the children?

Are there any areas where the children can hide, such as storage sheds?

Consider the following for your setting:

- Are gate fastenings at a level where a child cannot reach them? Are bolts and catches checked frequently to see that they are working properly? Are gates situated in the best area, opening away from and not blocking any access route for evacuation purposes?

- Are fences at a height where they cannot be climbed over by a child? If possible they should be constructed of a material which prevents passers-by putting items through;

- Do you have regular problems caused by other users such as the dropping of plastic bags, glass, litter etc? You may need to do check the outside areas throughout the day to ensure that the area remains safe throughout the time that the children are on site;

- Do you keep a cover on your sand pit when it is not in use, to avoid cat faeces becoming an issue?

Can the children come into contact with any poisonous plants or berries? Are there facilities for gardening and growing items in pots which the children can access?

Are there items such as rat traps used within the grounds? How do you ensure that children cannot come into contact with them? You would need to consider safe options such as a pre-baited sealed box, as you need to find a method that is child-friendly.

Something to think about

O Assessing the risk for different types of activities, for example more adults may be needed to supervise a swimming activity than a walk round a nearby field.

O The ages of the children on the outing and how children of different ages may change any associated risks.

O Involving older children in assessing the risks for being outside.

O Consideration for the setting when the premises are used by others too, such as community hall, when a pre-school may be using a part of the building.

Are there any problems relating to the weather such as slippery surfaces, waterlogged areas or non shaded areas on hot sunny days?

Are there ponds or water features within the outside area? Young children can drown in a small amount of water (refer to CAPT or ROSPA websites) and it is advisable not to have these in situ. However, in some circumstances, such as shared grounds, this is not possible. What preventative measures are in place to make sure that the children cannot gain access unsupervised? Are they securely fenced off and covered with mesh?

Are the children encouraged to feed the birds? You need to make sure that the children cannot pick up or eat any surplus nuts – as you may be responsible for a child with a nut allergy.

Are the outside toys and equipment safe for the children to use? Have portable items been assembled correctly? Is there adequate space between items of equipment to avoid collisions? Are safety mats/safety surfaces in place? It is always advisable to check for tripping hazards. Is safety bark used under equipment and if so, what action is taken to ensure that this remains at a suitable depth?

- Is equipment securely anchored to the ground?

- Do your swings have appropriate restraints?

- Are rules in place for the use of trampolines, such as the number of children allowed on the trampoline at any one time?

Outings and trips

Outings and trips should be planned in advance whenever possible. Parents should be advised when organised trips to a farm, for example, are planned. Written parental permission must be sought before any trips occur, whether to the local shops or park or further afield. If animals are involved such as visits to a sheep farm, all staff and accompanying adults should be told in advance as pregnant women should avoid contact with sheep during the lambing season because of the risk of miscarriage.

Staff need to make sure that they have risk assessed all parts of the outing. It is essential that an initial visit is made to assess any potential problems at the venue or along the route. A plan should be drawn up for dealing with these. Also a meeting point should be identified and all staff made aware of the procedure to follow in case of an emergency, such as child becoming lost.

It is important to know the location of the toilets and to ensure that children do not go into these without a member

of staff. Extra adults will be needed and management should take into account the age and stage of the children when allocating these and whether buggies and walking reins are needed.

A first aider should be amongst the staff. A first aid kit and any prescribed medication for an individual child should be taken, along with water, sun protection and sun hats and/or waterproofs as appropriate.

A register of all the children and adults taking part in the outing and the contact details of parents are essential.

If transport is used, management needed to be satisfied that the transport is fully insured. Making sure that the children alight on the pavement or an area of the car park away from other users, not the road; and appropriate restraints in vehicles, are other considerations.

The children should be prepared and told what they are going to see and to do at the venue. They need to be aware of the safety rules, boundaries and expectations of how to behave, for example, responding quickly to adults' directions and lining up without fuss. Also, if a play area is involved, they need to have the rules reiterated such as not going up the slide. Remember, this is not the usual environment which the children are used to.

If the outing is connected with a particular topic, the children may need some direction as to what to look for as they are bound to be excited at the novelty of being out in a group.

Section 3:
Making choices

In Section 1 of this book, we considered keeping children safe, primarily in relation to child protection, that is, abuse, in all of its forms. In Section 2 we explored the importance of the environment in keeping children safe.

This Section of the book has a focus on how we can support children in making choices about the things they would like to do, although, in reality, the things that children may choose to do may not be the safest choice! We will consider how, by making choices, children can feel that they have some control over their day, and how the wider work undertaken by settings with families can support children to become independent and confident learners. We will also consider how settings can meet their statutory obligations to keeping children safe.

Behaviour plays a large part in each child's development, and children need to understand the rules of the setting, which should be designed to keep everyone safe. Explanations are crucial, whether these are verbal or by the use of symbols or pictures to help children understand the message.

Children can play a part in helping to keep themselves safe. Babies have no concept of what is safe, so they need constant supervision. Older children's concept of danger depends on their age, development stage and their level of skill. Toddlers and under threes have little idea of safety issues and children aged three to five have only a limited understanding. Older children need to be made aware of the safety issues and the consequences of their behaviour, for example, throwing sand at each other and pushing, kicking or tripping others up during rough and tumble play.

So, it is important that adults:

- Set an example and be good role models for the children;

- Minimise hazards as far as possible by carrying out risk assessments;

- Be consistent – do not change the rules;

- Reinforce and repeat simple safety messages such as holding onto the hand rail when climbing or descending stairs;

- Show children how to handle items such as scissors and other equipment and apparatus properly and safely;

- Explain what may be dangerous, and why;

> 'We start teaching children from a young age about cause and effect – and they begin to understand that their behaviour can have an effect on others. Adults need to ensure that they are giving adequate supervision according to the activity and setting rules and boundaries that are achievable. Children also need explanations as to why they can and cannot do something'. Jubilee Day Nursery, West Berkshire

- Explain why some behaviour is unacceptable, and why;

- Demonstrate good safety practice;

- Praise and encourage appropriate behaviour;

- Try to ensure that children do not get into difficult and confrontational situations;

- Ask the children to say 'sorry' if they have done something wrong towards another child and if the child does so, acknowledge this positively.

Remember, children will respond to a positive approach. Think about the language you use, the way in which you guide children in their behaviour, and how you consider the reasons for certain behaviours. Not all of these are linked to possible abusive situations, as described in Section 1 of this book, but may be caused by other factors in a child's life. Knowledge of child development and the stage at which a particular child has reached, may help you to understand why they are displaying a particular unwanted behaviour. The level of a child's understanding and language development play a key part in this.

Most children display attention seeking behaviour at some point. However, when a child becomes disruptive, defiant, jealous, isolating themselves, become withdrawn or aggressive, the adult does need to respond as their safety may be an issue.

Behaviours may be a result of a child just not feeling well, and not being able to express that; behaviour can also be a result of a child who may be at risk from abuse, and showing reaction through their behaviour, such as aggression. Always consider the causes of behaviour as well as managing that behaviour. Remember that some children need support to manage their behaviour.

Child development

Staff working directly with children should have knowledge about child development, so they can identify, and act upon, concerns about a child. Working with parents in the best interests of their child should be a priority for the practitioner. When written observations are shared with parents, practitioners can use the information recorded to help parents understand how their child is developing, and to respond to any concerns the parents may have about their child's development.

When there are concerns about a child's welfare, records must be kept to show that the setting is, at least, monitoring the situation.

1. Children's records should be clear and concise – giving the facts.

2. Some difficulties noted may be linked to abuse, and this should be recognised also. For example, a child may become withdrawn and be less responsive than normal to the practitioner. This child may have been affected by something that is happening to them, and their change of behaviour could be an indicator.

SCENARIO

A small group of four year olds are sitting round a table playing a Lotto card game. Each child has several turns. Then, one child realises that he has not matched as many cards as others, so when it is his turn, he turns up more than one card. Another child looks upset and leaves the table; one other decides he is cheating and an argument breaks out. The children are becoming aggressive towards each other.

What should you do?

Think about:

O How could the adult have prevented this happening? (Effective strategies before a game starts – chatting with the children, ensuring they know the rules prior to staring the game, being near enough to step in and guide the play if needed).

O How can the adult now diffuse the situation? (Encouraging the children to talk about their feelings and possibly why it happened. Re-start the game, and join in too, to show how much fun can be had).

3. Staff should think about the child in a holistic way – not just focusing on one incident. What is happening in the child's life? Are their family factors to consider? Let's consider the wider picture when there are concerns about a child and their family.

Common Assessment Framework

Information sourced from the Department for Education website (www.education.gov.uk/childrenandyoungpeople/strategy/integratedworking/caf/).

The Common Assessment Framework (CAF) is a four-step process whereby practitioners can identify a child's needs early, assess those needs holistically, deliver coordinated services and review progress. The CAF is designed to be used when:

● a practitioner is worried about how well a child is progressing, for example, concerns about their health, development, welfare, their behaviour, their progress in learning or any other aspect of their wellbeing;

● a child, or their parent, raises a concern with a practitioner;

● a child's needs are unclear, or broader than the setting's service can address.

The CAF process is entirely voluntary and informed consent is mandatory, so families do not have to engage and, if they do, they can choose what information they want to share.

The CAF process is not a 'referral' process but a 'request for services' that will help a child and their family with the situation they are in.

So, what does the Common Assessment Framework look like?

The key point is that the child is at the heart of the assessment. The triangle represents the child's life in terms of their family circumstances, relationships with their

Assessment Framework

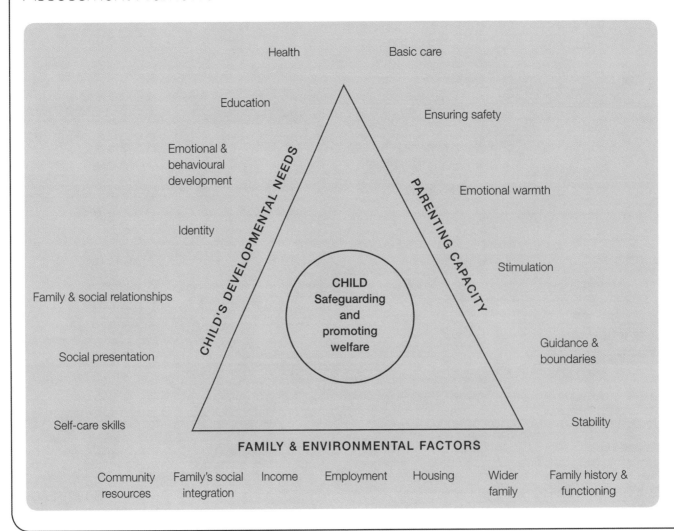

parents as well as considerations around the child's care and development needs.

For further information and training on the Common Assessment Framework, contact your Early Years Adviser within your local authority, who will be able to guide you.

The Common Core Skills and Knowledge

Information sourced from the Department for Education website, under National Archives (webarchive.national archives.gov.uk). The Common Core Skills and Knowledge for the Childcare Workforce is relevant to the work of practitioners, and can be found on the Department for Education Website, under National Archives.

What is the common core?

The common core describes the basic skills and knowledge that everyone working with children or young people is expected to have. It sets out six key areas of expertise and the skills needed in each of them. The common core gives all of us a common set of basic skills and knowledge. This will help practitioners to work together better, speak a common language and support children more effectively.

There are six areas we all need be aware of:

Effective communication and engagement with children and families
Good communication is central to establishing trust, and making sure information is shared and received in the way you intend. This key area highlights the importance of knowing how to listen, empathise, explain, consult, and seek support.

Child development
Understanding the developmental changes children and young people go through can be key to interpreting their behaviour. This area of expertise helps us to understand what makes children and young people think and act in the way they do, and to encourage us to respond to and support their needs as they emerge. Sound knowledge of child development is at the heart of a child carer's work.

Safeguarding and promoting the welfare of children
This set of skills centres on keeping children and young people safe, and knowing how to identify if they are suffering harm or neglect. They also help us to see when children and young people are not achieving their potential and help us to ensure their well-being and quality of life.

Supporting transitions
When children and young people go through change, it can have a profound effect on their behaviour and well-being. These skills help us to identify transitions, understand their likely impact and support children, young people and their families through them.

Multi-agency and integrated working
This key area describes the skills we need to work together effectively with people from different professional backgrounds. It highlights the importance of valuing individual expertise and of understanding the tools and processes that support multiagency and integrated working.

Information sharing
Knowing how and when to share information is an essential part of delivering better services for children. The skills and knowledge outlined in this area include understanding and respecting the legislation and ethics surrounding confidentiality and security of information.

When things go wrong for a child and their family, the consequences can be far reaching. Let's look at a case study (overleaf) relating to a child who attended a day nursery, and his mother's relationship with the staff of the setting.

CASE STUDY: RELATIONSHIPS WITH PARENTS

Background

The tragic death of a 2-year-old boy in January 2011 from multiple injuries, was later determined to be the result of separate incidents, with several major injuries being sustained over a period of days. The boy's mother was convicted of murder in respect of the child.

Concerns about the family and the child had been raised previously by a number of agencies, and the serious case review following the child's death found that opportunities to protect the child had been missed – significant opportunities were missed in the last few weeks of his life – at a child protection medical in the autumn of 2010, following concerns about a burn to his foot, between Christmas 2010 and New Year 2011 when the child attended his two year developmental check and finally in early January, when his nursery were concerned about bruises, raised their concerns with his mother, but did not report their concerns to the social care team.

Three days later he died.

The review that followed made comments about the nursery: 'The staff in the nursery did not proactively exchange information about the child internally and had no contact with any other professionals or agency. The interactions described with the child's mother appear to be 'chats' initiated by the mother when she wanted to talk to someone. There is no sense of direct or purposeful work being undertaken in accordance with a plan for the child. This child was one among fifty children being looked after at the nursery'.

Learning point

In many ways the 'rule of optimism' seemed to be affecting the professionals.

Research evidence shows that "efforts to think the best of families" were found in a 2005-07 study which noted that "There was reluctance among many practitioners to make negative professional judgments about a parent. " In this case, the longstanding use of the same nursery by the child's mother, extended family and by the mother herself (she had attended it as a child) may have led to a familiarity which clouded the views of the professionals of the mother's capacity to care for her son. The mother, when interviewed, referred to the staff as 'more like friends'.

The child had been seen by staff in the nursery early in the New Year 2011 with a number of marks and bruises on his body and was described as 'distressed'. No referral was made and clear guidelines and procedures were not followed as staff believed the explanations put forward by the mother and therefore did not take action to protect the child'.

What appears to be central to this may have been the responses given by the mother to the staff at the nursery – just how plausible were her explanations in respect of her son's injuries? With the child already 'known' to local agencies – why would nursery staff not take action and report their concerns?

The crucial point here is that 'clear guidelines and procedures were not followed'.

When staff accept their responsibilities in protecting children, which is made very clear in universal safeguarding training, they should have no hesitation in seeking advice, at the very least, or making a referral. It is worth repeating that, regardless of the feelings of the practitioner, the child must come first. It is better that an investigation takes place to safeguard a child, even if there appears to be a lack of evidence.

If we think about a child and the child's family in a holistic way, we can build up a jigsaw picture of the child and the people around the child – many pieces that represent the whole. If there are concerns about a child in the setting, even if the information seems insignificant, the concerns must be reported, as they contribute to the overall jigsaw picture – it may be that the information shared completes the overall picture allowing the social worker team to intervene to protect the child at the earliest opportunity.

Any concerns raised by a practitioner about a child's welfare must not be dismissed, equally, the designated person has clear responsibilities in keeping children safe from harm too. Training specific to this role is made available through Local Authorities, and Ofsted will check at inspection whether all staff have attended universal training as well as confirming that the designated person has attended their own training. Often, the designated person for child protection has the responsibility for the CAF too.

When practitioners have concerns about a child, they should, whenever possible, raise the concerns with the parents, unless to do so may place the child at greater risk. When parents are asked about injuries practitioners notice on a child, a record must be made of the date, time, question asked and response given. This procedure is standard and should be in the policies and procedure documents for the setting. Parents must be aware that these procedures are in the best interests of the child, the setting and for themselves too. This information would be recorded on an incident sheet which should not be confused with an accident sheet.

Children will injure themselves at times when they are outside of the setting, and explanations from parents will satisfy you. There may be occasions when you feel less happy about the response from the parents and may even feel uncomfortable. If a child is old enough and able to tell you themselves what has happened to cause, for example, bruising, you may record that too, and accept, with no further action, that your written record is sufficient. The parent needs to sign any form or record you complete about their child, and the date must be shown too.

When parents indicate either through their own behaviour or language that something is 'not quite right', this needs recording too, as there may be a problem that needs addressing. If a parent avoids you, changes the subject, makes little eye contact or demonstrates in any other way that they would prefer not to engage with you, this could be an indicator of a problem.

Being over familiar with a family can have serious consequences – it is not good practice to become friends with the families you work with. Once a culture of friendship in embedded in practice, this is would be hard to reverse. Parents need to understand that your relationships with them are professional and friendly, but that you are not actually friends with them. Guard against social networking with the families you work with, and at all times, keep professional boundaries in place.

In the case of this mother, nursery staff believed the explanations of injuries given were genuine and they accepted what they heard. They were, however, not alone – the mother had given explanations to others too – for example, at the hospital, where medical staff were given plausible reasons for injuries. The child had been taken to hospital with burns and blisters on his foot, but his mother said it was from a radiator he slept near, which was accepted by police and health workers.

Sharing any information from parents when there are concerns is very important. The primary role of the practitioner is to safeguard children from harm and develop skills to work professionally with families in the best interests of the child. Practitioners need to avoid being overly optimistic about parents, and being misled by them. Amongst other things, this comes through a proper understanding of risk factors; clear procedures, and high quality supervision which challenges practitioners' thinking. This is a priority in early years settings which deliver a high quality service.

When we think about protecting children, the CAF and family support, we need to focus on our own skills and knowledge – the way we observe, collate and assess information and detect patterns where there may be issues of neglect and physical abuse – this must become a part of basic good practice in any nursery setting.

So, how can the Common Core help you in your work? Let's focus on 3 areas of the common core – safeguarding and promoting the welfare of children; multi-agency, and integrated working and information sharing.

For leaders of settings

The information below can be used in your team meetings to help you identify which staff may need additional training to help them in their work with both children and their families.

Reminder: Those who work with children have a responsibility to safeguard and promote their welfare. This is an important responsibility and requires vigilance. You need to be able to recognise when a child may not be achieving to their developmental potential or their health may be impaired, and be able to identify appropriate sources of help for them and their families. It is important to identify concerns as early as possible so that children, their families can get the help they need. As well as ensuring that children are free from harm, it is equally important to ensure their well-being and quality of life.

Consider, as a team, how effective are we in:

1. Establishing respectful, trusting relationships with children and their families?

2. Understanding what is meant by safeguarding and the different ways in which children can be harmed (including by other children and young people)?

3. Making considered judgements about how to act to safeguard and promote a child's welfare, where appropriate consulting with the child, parent or carer to inform our thinking?

4. Giving the child the opportunity to participate in decisions affecting them, as appropriate to their age and ability and taking their wishes and feelings into account?

5. Understanding the key role of parents and carers in safeguarding and promoting children's welfare and involve them accordingly, while recognising factors that can affect parenting and increase the risk of abuse (for example, domestic violence)?

6. Understanding that signs of abuse can be subtle and be expressed in play, artwork and in the way children approach relationships with other children and/or adults?

All staff need to be clear about the importance of record keeping, and to be able to develop their skills in making effective observations. Reporting should make a distinction between observation, facts, information gained from others, and opinion. Staff should be undertaking on-going assessments of children and be alert to concerns about a child safety or welfare, including unexplained changes in behaviour and signs of abuse or neglect. Through training, staff should be able to recognise when a child or young person is in danger or at risk of harm, and take action to protect them. Records should be based on real facts and not be influenced by personal beliefs or feelings.

New, or less experienced staff, may need support to gain confidence to represent the child and his or her rights. They may need to develop the confidence to challenge their own and others' practice too. Some staff may also need support and guidance in how they can develop and maintain appropriate professional relationships with children.

Everyone working in the setting should have knowledge of the most current legislation, for example, the recently introduced requirement about the use of phones and cameras in settings. Staff should also have information about the Local Safeguarding Children Board and its role.

Managers will need to know when, and how, to discuss concerns with parents. They need to understand the roles of other agencies, local procedures on child protection, and appreciate the necessity of information sharing within the context of children's well-being and safety.

For staff to know the boundaries of their personal responsibilities, knowing when to involve others, and knowing where to get advice and support, is a major consideration. Staff may witness upsetting situations and need to know how to get support and who to speak to, without breaching confidentality.

Reminder: Multi-agency working is about different services, agencies and teams of professionals and other staff working together to provide the services that fully meet the needs of children and their parents or carers. To work successfully on a multi-agency basis you need to be clear about your own role and aware of the roles of other professionals, you need to be confident about your own standards and targets and respectful of those that apply to other services, actively seeking and respecting the knowledge and input others can make to delivering best outcomes for children. These behaviours should apply across the public, private and voluntary sectors.

Consider, as a team, how effective are we:

1. In communicating with other practitioners and professionals? Do we listen and ensure that we are being listened to? Do we respond clearly and professionally when we are approached by other agencies? Are we confident in seeking help from others?

2. In providing timely, appropriate, succinct information to enable other practitioners to deliver their support to the child, parent or carer?

Something to think about

O How the home and family circumstances of individual children may affect their behaviour and use this information to deal effectively with difficult situations.

O Information and detail about children and their families should only be shared with people who have a right to have it, that is, your lead practitioner, supervisor or manager, an external agency.

O Follow agreed procedures for recording, storing and sharing information.

---

3. In recording, sharing and feeding back information, using IT skills where necessary to do so?

4. In working in a team context, forging and sustaining relationships across agencies and respecting the contribution of others working with children and their families?

Settings need to be proactive, for example, in the way in which they take the necessary actions to protect children. This may be by making a referral, or seeking advice through the local children's services at the earliest opportunity. Staff should be encouraged to ask questions about the process used to report concerns about a child, so that they may have confidence both in the process and any appropriate action taken, where necessary, for the benefit of the child.

Settings should be able to decide when they should provide the support themselves and when they should refer the situation to another practitioner or professional. Seeking advice when there are concerns about a child, can provide settings with reassurance that they are following correct procedures to safeguard the child.

Settings can contribute to whatever actions are needed to safeguard children and to assist in any review undertaken in relation to a child's welfare.

Checklist

Do we:

1. Know our main jobs and responsibilities within our working environment?

2. Know the value and expertise we bring to a team and that brought by each of our colleagues?

3. Develop our skills and knowledge with training from experts, to minimise the need for referral to specialist services, enabling continuity for the family and child?

4. Have a general knowledge and understanding of the range of organisations and individuals working with children and those caring for them, and are we all aware of the roles and responsibilities of other professionals?

5. Know what to do in given cases, e.g. for referrals or raising concerns?

6. Know what the triggers are for reporting incidents or unexpected behaviour?

7. Know how to work within our own and other organisational values, beliefs and cultures?

8. Know what to do when there is an insufficient response from other organisations or agencies, while maintaining a focus on what is in the child's best interests?

Reminder: Sharing information in a timely and accurate way is an essential part of helping to deliver better services to children and their families. Indeed, sometimes it will help save lives. Practitioners in different agencies should work together and share information for the safety and well-being of children. It is also important to understand and respect issues and legislation surrounding the control and confidentiality of information. It is important to build trust from the outset by clarifying issues and procedures surrounding confidentiality and information sharing. Practitioners must adopt the right approach to information sharing by following the correct procedures and by ensuring that the child, parent or carer understands the process.

Staff working with children, and their families, need to use clear language to communicate information; to be able to listen and to be able to check understanding. It is important for families that settings create an environment of trust, by seeking consent where possible and appropriate, and in this way emphasising respect for the child and their family. Encourage families to share information where appropriate, ensuring that they understand why it is important to do so.

While we think about the need to share information in the best interests of a child, staff should consider the implications of not doing so. Staff need to understand that consent is not always necessary to share information, even where information is confidential in nature. It may be shared without consent in certain circumstances (for example, where the child is at risk of harm or there is a legal obligation to disclose).

Families can naturally become frustrated if they are being repeatedly asked to provide the same information over and over again, so settings should understand that it is not always necessary to collect information directly from families. Staff should be aware that information can often be gathered from other sources, such as health visitors and other professionals involved with a family.

Checklist

Do we:

1. Know who to share information with and when; understand the difference between information sharing on individual, organisational and professional levels?

2. Know how to share information in writing, by telephone, electronically or in person?

3. Know what to record, how to dispose of records correctly and when to feed back or follow up?

4. Make sure we are always aware of own (and others') professional boundaries?

5. Know that different types of information exist (for example, confidential information, personal data and sensitive personal data), and appreciate the implications of those differences?

6. Appreciate the effect of cultural and religious beliefs; refrain from making assumptions about certain cultures or backgrounds?

7. As far as possible, make clear to the parent or carer how the information they provide will be used?

In 2011, the Department for Education and the Department for Health ministers established a 'task and finish' group to:

- explore and reflect on how exemplar information-sharing practices in the early years already in train in many local areas can be further promoted;

- identify any on-going barriers which different local partners experience to information sharing in the early years;

- make recommendations about how barriers to information sharing might be overcome.

The work of the 'task and finish' group was carried out through a series of three full group meetings, rounds of separate one-one discussions and interviews and several case study visits. This evidence fed into the report Information Sharing in the Foundation Years: a report from the task and finish group.

Examples of local tools to support best practice which are referred to in the report are available at www.foundation years.org.uk/information-sharing. On the opposite page, you will see a Model for Information Sharing.

Supporting children in making choices

We have considered the need for effective engagement with children and their families and we have explored ways in which we can share information in the best interests of children.

When we effectively engage with children, involving them in decisions that affect them on a day to day basis, we know that we are supporting them across all areas of their learning.

Knowledge of child development in the Early Years Foundation Stage is central to the work of the practitioner.

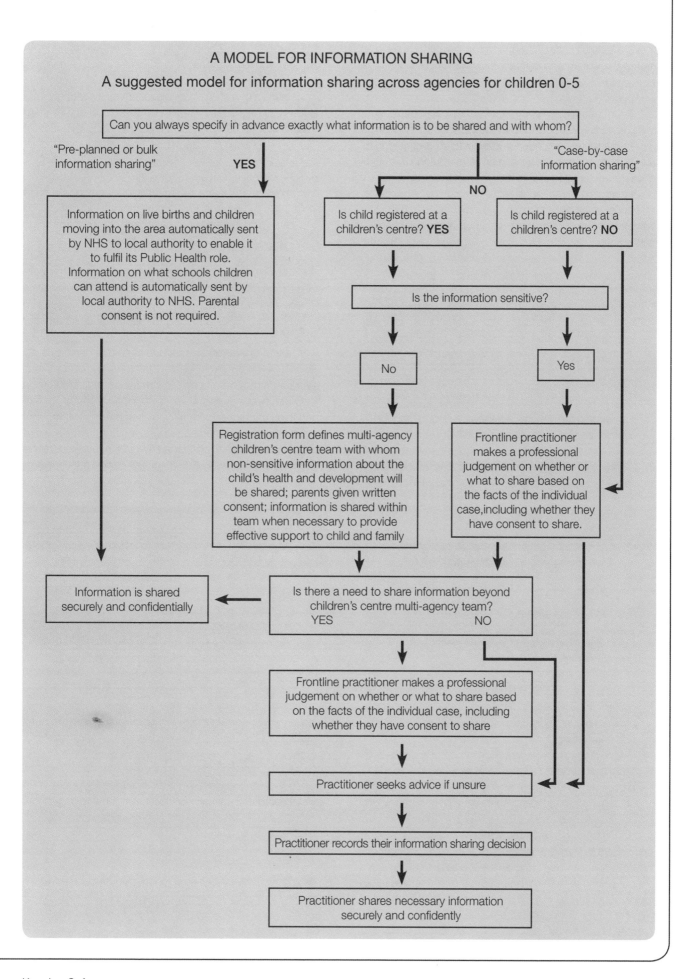

A MODEL FOR INFORMATION SHARING

A suggested model for information sharing across agencies for children 0-5

Can you always specify in advance exactly what information is to be shared and with whom?

"Pre-planned or bulk information sharing"

YES

"Case-by-case information sharing"

NO

Information on live births and children moving into the area automatically sent by NHS to local authority to enable it to fulfil its Public Health role. Information on what schools children can attend is automatically sent by local authority to NHS. Parental consent is not required.

Is child registered at a children's centre? YES

Is child registered at a children's centre? NO

Is the information sensitive?

No

Yes

Registration form defines multi-agency children's centre team with whom non-sensitive information about the child's health and development will be shared; parents given written consent; information is shared within team when necessary to provide effective support to child and family

Frontline practitioner makes a professional judgement on whether or what to share based on the facts of the individual case, including whether they have consent to share.

Information is shared securely and confidentially

Is there a need to share information beyond children's centre multi-agency team?
YES   NO

Frontline practitioner makes a professional judgement on whether or what to share based on the facts of the individual case, including whether they have consent to share

Practitioner seeks advice if unsure

Practitioner records their information sharing decision

Practitioner shares necessary information securely and confidently

In order to fully support children in their learning and in meeting their needs, practitioners need to know how children learn as well as what they learn under in the Prime and Specific areas of learning in the EYFS.

It is crucial that practitioners have knowledge of the physical, intellectual, linguistic, social and emotional growth and development of babies and children. Of course, it is difficult to determine specific times when developmental changes occur, as these will differ from person to person.

What is important is a basic understanding of those changes and how they can affect a baby or child's behaviour. Parents and carers may be well placed to identify developmental and behavioural changes in their children but they may also find them difficult to cope with and seek reassurance, information, advice and support at various stages.

Important elements of observation

How confident are you in:

1. How you observe a child's behaviour, understand its context, and notice any unexpected changes?

2. Listening actively and respond to concerns expressed about developmental or behavioural changes?

3. Recording observations in an appropriate manner?

4. Your understanding that babies and children see and experience the world in different ways?

5. Evaluating the situation, taking into consideration the individual, their situation and development issues?

6. Being able to recognise the signs of a possible developmental delay?

7. Being able to support children with a developmental difficulty or disability, and understand that their families, parents and carers will also need support and reassurance?

8. Making considered decisions on whether concerns can be addressed by providing or signposting additional sources of information or advice?

The EYFS (card 1.3) reminds us that 'giving children choice helps them to learn that while there are several different options, they can only choose one at a time. Children who are supported to make choices learn that sometimes they can have, or do, something now, while at other times they may have to wait longer for a particular choice. Making choices about things such as what they will do or what they

will wear helps children feel some sense of control over their day. Choice sometimes includes choosing not to do something, such as choosing not to join in when everybody else is moving to music'!

So, how can we help children to make choices? Babies can be provided with opportunities to make choices in their play and explorations of the environment. When you offer a range of play that babies can access, such as textured mats, brightly coloured toys and musical equipment, babies will show their interest by reaching out or crawling towards the item. As children grow in confidence, they will explore their environment more actively and will require good supervision, as they do not understand the dangers around them.

It is at this stage that the adult needs to introduce the concept of 'boundaries', whether these are physical or by way of clear explanations. Just saying 'no' to a child is meaningless. Children need to gain an understanding of why they are not allowed to do something, and this is when choice comes into the equation.

Striking the balance between giving children choice and keeping them safe is not always easy, as children will be keen to do what they have chosen to do and the adult will be equally keen to keep the child safe!

Assessing risk is one way of determining whether the child may or may not do something. As children reach a stage of development where they can appreciate dangers, such as climbing to a height that could result in injury, they can be given time to think about what could happen, and as well as to what they could do to keep safe, such as to wear suitable footwear for the climbing, and not to climb too high.

Giving children time to talk about the things they would like to do is important. Allow them to express themselves to show you what interests them, and support them in their choices, even if that means that you need to put safety measures in place first.

Supporting children's independence is crucial within their early years. Allow babies and children to do the things can manage with ease and then provide support to help them with the things they cannot quite manage.

Children need to understand that we all have to make choices at times, and that we cannot always have what we want at the time we wanted it! This can be hard for children to understand, after all, their view is simple – I want to do this, and I want to do this now! It may be that the adult has to explain that the time may not be right, for example, the adult may have to say 'We cannot do this now, as we have to get the table ready for lunch, but we will do it as soon

as we can when lunch is finished'. When children are given explanations as to why they cannot do something, they are more likely to accept the situation.

As children develop, they may have more in depth discussions with each other and the adults responsible for them. They can talk about the things that make them feel good about themselves, the people who can help them, how they can keep themselves safe, how they can recognise and avoid possible danger, their reasons for making particular choices and explore the reasons why they are allowed to do or to have some things, and not other things.

FINDING THE BALANCE

At Woodlands Day Nursery staff acknowledge that there is a fine line between allowing children to take risks and being overprotective.

'Striking a balance between being aware of the dangers that children in our care may be faced with, and being over protective of them because of the fear of these dangers becoming a reality, is always a difficult balance to achieve, however we feel it is vital if we are to support children in their development. Firstly, it is of the upmost importance for us to know what dangers the children may be faced with. This includes not only the daily health and safety issues that can arise within the nursery setting but also dangers that the children may be faced with outside the setting. Within the nursery setting, but it is important to recognise the concern, i.e. when giving children scissors to use or when providing a 'risk-taking' environment outside, such as climbing; it is important to recognise whether these concerns need to be addressed through the boundaries being set for the child, or by the child learning the boundary by themselves. Certain boundaries need to be established for children to avoid harm, such as modelling what we use certain equipment for, i.e. knives and scissors, however with regards to other boundaries such as adventurous play it is important to allow children to take risks and recognise the dangers themselves so that they are able to set their own boundaries. We believe that if children aren't provided with the opportunities to recognise dangers independently then they won't learn to see the dangers as they grow older. We believe it is important when setting boundaries to give reasons for these and most importantly 'real' reasons that the children can relate to. If the child can understand why these boundaries are present they will, more often than not, respect them, leading to learning that is safe but allows children to take risks and recognise dangers themselves'.

CASE STUDY: JUBILEE DAY NURSERY

Jubilee Day Nursery has a pre-school that provides daily activities for the children to enable them to routinely take risks in their play. The children are shown in easy stages how to climb a five bar gate or tree, with support and encouragement; the children master the skill and grow in confidence, the staff are always on hand to assist, the children then begin to help their friends.

When outside the children talk about safety when walking, from roads and stranger awareness to stinging nettles and what berries are good to eat and what are not. Children pick their own blackberries and learn for themselves about the risk of the brambles – this helps the children understand there is a consequence to the actions they take.

The children are able to explore the outside with the confidence that there is someone on hand to help and support and show them rather than saying 'No! Don't do that! You may hurt yourself!'

Inside the nursery, children are encouraged to be independent at meal times by pouring their own drinks, preparing their own snacks and making sandwiches. Staff demonstrate how to use a knife safely and guide support and encourage children.

Staff try and use real tools and materials, as much as possible, both inside and out and teach the children to do things safely and responsibly whilst learning and having fun.

Under twos at Jubilee Day Nursery

All children are encouraged to 'learn by doing' from a very early age. Risk-taking opportunities are always available from being shown how to climb down stairs to climbing onto soft play, logs and planks. The children are shown, guided and supported and praise given to them helping them to become confident and independent in their play.

On walks to the woods although some of the younger children wear reins, as road safety is a big feature of the trip – listening out for cars and looking both ways. All children who walk wear high visibility jackets. The younger children climb up banks and are taught to look out for tree roots to minimise trips and falls.

At breakfast time the children pour their own cereal by scooping it out with a cup. They start to learn knife control by buttering their own bread once a week, with a little help from an adult. The children are made aware of temperatures in food for example by blowing on their food to cool it down.

The children have toys and equipment inside and out which promote risk-taking this is supported by the staff.

Forest schools at Jubilee Day Nursery

The aim at the nursery is to avoid being overprotective of the children. Forest schools support this ethos as the children are able to take risks for themselves whilst in the woods. The children know and understand the forest school rules and discuss them at the beginning and end of each session. This gives them a clear knowledge of their boundaries.

The children are shown how to use tools safely and how to look after them including carrying them and safe storage. The children make lots of natural objects using saws knives and often make fires to cook on. The staff ensure the children have fun and learn new experiences with an awareness to risks and danger of their environment but to have the confidence always to try new things and extend their own learning. All of the children benefit from the forest school approach. They thrive in the outdoor environment. It contributes to their all round development.

The Rights of the Child (source Unicef)

In 1989, governments worldwide promised all children the same rights by adopting the UN Convention on the Rights of the Child. These rights are based on what a child needs to survive, grow, participate and fulfil their potential. They apply equally to every child, regardless of who they are, or where they are from.

The Convention says that every child has:

- The right to a **childhood** (including protection from harm)

- The right to be **educated** (including all girls and boys completing primary school)

- The right to be **healthy** (including having clean water, nutritious food and medical care)

- The right to be treated **fairly** (including changing laws and practices that are unfair on children)

- The right to be **heard** (including considering children's views).

The role of the practitioner is to support the learning of each child, meet their needs and to keep them safe.

Checklist

Indoors

- Does your indoor environment provide a safe, secure yet challenging space for children?

- Does your indoor environment contain resources which are appropriate, well maintained and accessible for all young children?

- Are indoor spaces planned so that they can be used flexibly and an appropriate range of activities is provided for the younger children?

- Does your indoor provision meet the needs of all the children as a place to feel 'at home'?

Outside

- Do all staff recognise that being outside has a positive impact on children's sense of wellbeing and helps in all aspects of children's development?

- How do staff create opportunities for doing things in different ways and on different scales than when indoors?

- What opportunities do the young children have to experience the seasons and the natural world around them?

- How are the young children able to explore, use their senses, and be physically active?

Example Incident Report Form (supplied by Jubilee Day Nursery)

INCIDENT REPORT FORM   PRIVATE AND CONFIDENTIAL

Date and time of incident:

_____

Name(s) of child/children/person(s) involved in incident:

_____

Name of person reporting incident:

_____

Where the incident took place:

_____

What happened:

_____

_____

_____

_____

_____

_____

Witness to incident:

_____

Action(s) taken by:

_____

_____

_____

_____

Parent informed by: Date and time:

_____

Parent signature:

_____

Manager/Deputy signature:

_____

Accident Record Form (supplied by Jubilee Day Nursery)

ACCIDENT REPORT FORM

Name of child:

Date and time of incident:

Location of accident:

Cause of accident

Injury sustained:

Treatment given:

Dealt with by:
Signature

Witness by:
Signature

Reported to Manager/Deputy:
Signature Manager/Deputy:

Parents name:
Signature:

Incident form completed: YES / NO

Riddor form completed: YES / NO

Example Minor Accident Record Sheet (supplied by Jubilee Day Nursery)

MINOR ACCIDENT RECORD SHEET

Child's Name:

Sheet number:

DATE	TIME OF ACCIDENT	CAUSE OF ACCIDENT	INJURY SUSTAINED AND TREATMENT GIVEN	WHO DEALT WITH THE ACCIDENT	WITNESS TO ACCIDENT	PARENT NAME AND SIGNATURE	MANAGER/ DEPUTY MANAGER NAME AND SIGNATURE

Bringing it all together

Children only know what they experience. When they feel safe and secure, they respond and thrive. For children who have had unhappy experiences due to the way they have been treated, their lives may be adversely affected for many years.

Anyone who works with babies, young children and their families, have a duty to meet each child's care and learning needs. There is no greater responsibility than to care for children, and to make their childhood as happy and carefree as possible.

The care environment should provide rich opportunities for children to develop – children need spaces that allow them to confidently play alongside others and learn.

Working with parents to ensure consistency is important. There is a strong expectation within the EYFS for settings to work in partnership with parents in the best interests of children. Parents want to know that their children are being well cared for in their absence – that everyone working in the setting has the children's safety and welfare at the heart of their work.

Remember to:

1. Acknowledge that the parents are the child's primary educators. The role of the practitioner is to support parents by developing professional relationships with them.

2. Assign a key person to each child who should work to form a warm, trusting, respectful relationship with that child and their family.

3. Work with them to enhance their child's life. Establish an ongoing dialogue with parents to ensure that early concerns can be acted upon.

There is conclusive research evidence that the commitments of the EYFS to support children are central to improving the quality of care for all children.

References and acknowledgements

References

Early Years Foundation Stage Statutory Framework 2014 (Department for Education, www.gov.uk/dfe)

Government's statutory guidance 'Working Together to Safeguard Children 2013' (www.gov.uk/government/publications/working-together-to-safeguard-children)

Information Sharing in the Foundation Years: a report from the task and finish group, available online from www.foundationyears.org.uk

NSPCC (www.nspcc.co.uk)

Ofsted (www.ofsted.gov.uk)

UNICEF (www.unicef.org).

Acknowledgements

With grateful thanks to the following:

Jubilee Day Nursery, West Berkshire

Woodlands Day Nursery, West Berkshire

Sue Robb, Head of Early Years, 4 Children, Children and Family Charity

Sally Hogg, Development Manager for Children Under One, NSPCC

Sheila Collins, retired childcare professional.

NOTES